METEORS

METEORS

MORE MUSINGS BY AN
ASTRONOMER WHO
BECAME A PSYCHIATRIST

JAIME SMITH

GRANVILLE ISLAND
PUBLISHING

Publisher's Cataloging-in-Publication data
Names: Smith, Jaime, author.
Title: Meteors : more musings by an astronomer who became a psychiatrist / Jaime Smith.
Description: Includes index. | Vancouver Island, Vancouver: Granville Island Publishing Ltd., 2023.
Identifiers: ISBN: 978-1-989467-62-6 (paperback) | 978-1-989467-63-3 (ebook)
Subjects: LCSH Smith, Jaime. | Astronomers--Biography. | Psychiatrists--Canada--Biography. | Space and time--Philosophy. | Philosophy--Essays. | Science--Essays. | BISAC BIOGRAPHY & AUTOBIOGRAPHY / Personal Memoirs | SCIENCE / Essays | PHILOSOPHY / Essays | LITERARY COLLECTIONS / Essays
Classification: LCC RC438.6 .S65 2023 | DDC 616.89/0092--dc23

Editor: Jessica Kaplan
Copy editor: Rebecca Coates
Designer: Paul DuVernet, Mica Design

Granville Island Publishing Ltd.
Tel: 604-688-0320
Toll free: 1-877-688-0320
info@granvilleislandpublishing.com
www.granvilleislandpublishing.com

For Jack, Joel, Peggy and David – they all helped

CONTENTS

BELIEF

SELF AND SOCIETY

SOCIETY AND SELF

SOUNDS AND WORDS

TIME PAST

TIME PRESENT

TIME FUTURE

EPILOGUE

ACKNOWLEDGEMENTS

INDEX

AUTHOR'S NOTE

I thought of naming this book of essays *Comets* but decided that since comets, although visually attractive, are really only dirty icebergs, that wouldn't be appealing. Meteors, on the other hand, the brief but brilliant "shooting stars" seen in the skies after dark, seemed appropriate, though they are only small, glowing bits of cosmic rubbish, heated by friction with our atmosphere.

INTRODUCTION

After my second retirement, from the practice of psychiatry, in November 2009 (my first retirement was from professional astronomy in 1966), I enrolled in a continuing education course in Finnish at the University of Victoria, having always enjoyed learning languages. After three years I had mastered the grammatical intricacies of this non-Indo-European tongue, and with the help of a native speaker, I was able to read some Finnish and set about translating into English the 270-page detective novel *Katumurha (Street Murder)* by Jarkko Sipilä.

During these years I also kept a personal diary in Finnish, read books by other Finnish authors and even bought a copy of *Raamattu* (the Bible), to practise with familiar stories and sayings, like *Ei mitään uutta aurigon alla* (There's nothing new under the sun).

In 2012 and 2013 I made several visits to Helsinki, exploring the country by rail and rented car, from Karelia, along the southeastern border, adjacent to Russia, to above the Arctic Circle in Lapland. Afterwards, I was convinced that with just a few months of total immersion, I could easily adapt to living there and investigated the possibility of immigration. My retirement income was deemed adequate and as a grandchild of Finnish immigrants to North America, I was entitled to relocate there. However, with three daughters and seven grandsons all in British Columbia, I elected to stay put (even though the amenities for the elderly in Finland are superior to those in Canada).

For something completely different, I thought of learning another non-Indo-European language. Having coincidentally made the acquaintance of a new immigrant from the People's Republic of China, I decided to learn some Mandarin. Unlike Finnish, Mandarin grammar is "easy-peasy," much like English, but the pleremic written language is intricate and learning the meaning of each character is tedious. After three years of continuing education in Mandarin, learning how the characters are constructed and memorizing about a thousand, I had to admit that while I knew that I could learn to speak it readily with about six months of total immersion (offered in Shanghai at low cost), to read even a simple newspaper text would require rote learning of about four thousand characters. Feeling too old to travel and to live in Shanghai for half a year, I threw in the sponge. For a consolation prize, I bought a Finnish–Chinese dictionary in Helsinki.

I asked myself again, now what?

In the winter of 2018, I decided to write a memoir/autobiography for my family, compiling the past from travel notes, Christmas letters and a few excerpts from my diaries from earlier years. I self-published the book as *Foxtrot* (2020) and gave away about fifty copies to friends and relations.

Since I enjoyed the challenge of writing, and have enjoyed reading and learning since childhood, my eldest daughter, Annie, suggested I write and post blogs about topics that I found interesting. I began by writing about books and book reviews, posting them on my blogsite, karhunluola.com (*karhunluola* meaning "bear's cave" in Finnish). Once again, at the urging of friends and family, I published a collection of over 140 essays, together with a condensation of my previous memoir, in *Stardust: Memoir and Essays by an Astronomer Who Became a Psychiatrist* (2021).

The writing continued. Grist for the mill of essay writing continued to derive from my daily perusal of literary journals and reviews to which I subscribe, such as the *Times Literary Supplement,* the *London Review of Books,* the *New York Review of Books,* the *Guardian* and the magazine *Literary Review.* After four years, the corpus of posts now numbers 360. The 130 essays selected for this book, *Meteors,* were initially written and posted as blogs over the course of a year (2021) and focus on a broad array of themes, such as matter, life, the mind, belief, self, society and sounds and words. Running throughout the collection is also a focus on time: the past, the present and the future.

Not originally written with an eye to their categorization by chapter, each essay was individually composed, often in the period before falling asleep, during nocturnal awakenings by the muse Urania, or before arising in the predawn. After a light but wholesome breakfast in my quarters, I would begin composition of a first draft before noon, then review, revise and publish on my blog when satisfied. What emerged is a collection that reflects separate flashes of images or ideas, metaphoric meteors, combined to form an album of snapshots of my thoughts over this present time period. While some essays are related to past formative events, others are fearful visions of what lies ahead for humanity, as the horrors of warfare become eclipsed by our approach to the inescapable future event horizon — that of our self-induced annihilation.

MATTER

1

Cosmic Rubbish and Nomenclature

About 4.6 billion years ago, a cloud of interstellar dust coalesced by gravitation into a solar system consisting of a fairly ordinary star surrounded by planets (some large with one or more satellites) and an assortment of leftover rubbish called minor planets, or asteroids if substantial. Most of this leftover material resides scattered in orbits between Mars and Jupiter, the fourth and fifth planets, but some have more elliptical orbits that intersect those of the third planet, Earth.

Approximately 66 million years ago, one of these asteroids even crashed into our planet, causing the cretaceous extinction, a sudden mass obliteration of three-quarters of the plant and animal species on Earth, including all the dinosaurs. Although considered a relatively rare event, possible future collisions are nevertheless closely monitored by calculating the orbits of all known potential candidates.

Larger pieces of assorted cosmic debris, when smaller than minor planets, are given names by those that discover them (and report their findings), often amateur astronomers who scan the skies as a hobby. Selected names often celebrate scientists or others deemed worthy of respect, such as Ludwik Zamenhof, the inventor of the artificial language Esperanto, and even controversial political figures, like Eva Perón.

Distant, bright-appearing stars have historically often been given names of Arabic origin, like Altair or Aldebaran, that reflect their cataloguing by Arabian astronomers in the Middle Ages.

From antiquity to about 1750, apparent groupings of brighter stars led to the naming of eighty-eight constellations distributed around the celestial sphere. Often imaginary representations of mythological figures like Orion and Cassiopeia, some groupings are instead named for scientific instruments, like Telescopium and Microscopium in the night sky of the southern hemisphere. Not visible to European observers, these constellations were given their names by explorers who ventured below the equator.

The nearest star to us is the Sun, and its planets have traditionally been given names associated with gods of antiquity, the order of which — Sun, Mercury, Venus, Earth, Mars, (Asteroids), Jupiter, Saturn, Uranus, Neptune, Pluto — was once easily remembered by the mnemonic "so many very eager men ate juicy steaks using no plates." Of course, this now requires updating, for Pluto has been downgraded from a major to a minor planet due to its small size and extreme orbital eccentricity.

I once tried translating the English names of the planets to their Mandarin equivalents for a Chinese friend, using an online translation app, and he howled with laughter when I told him that the sixth planet from the sun was called Urine. (Beware of automated translations.)

July 1, 2021

2

RASCals and Meteors

The *Observer's Handbook* of the Royal Astronomical Society of Canada (RASC) has been published annually for 130 years. The current 2021 edition is a handy softbound 352-page veritable encyclopedia of information about what can be seen by those looking above their heads on a clear night, unaided or by using telescopes and binoculars. Within the pages of the handbook, professional astronomers have contributed brief but detailed notes and tables on observation techniques and astronomical phenomena, including time; optics and observation; eclipses; the moon, the sun, planets and satellites; dwarf and minor planets; meteors, comets and dust; stars; the deep sky; and comprehensive maps of the night sky.

The section on meteors in the 2021 handbook was contributed by Margaret Campbell-Brown and Peter Brown of Western University in London, Ontario, and consists of three pages of definitions and descriptions of the origins, observable phenomena, brightness and physical composition of meteors. The writing is accompanied by graphs of brightness vs. velocity, as well as the directional distribution of meteors over the sky, along with a tabulated list of meteor shower dates for the year.

I bought my first copy of the handbook, included in the modest price of a regular annual RASC membership, as a student of astronomy in 1951, and have periodically referred to it over the many years since then. There are chapters of RASCals (as we call ourselves) around the country that organize events such as lectures and "star parties," where groups of observers collectively meet, observe and photograph celestial objects. Many RASCals also have taken remarkable photographs of deep sky phenomena like nebulae and galaxies, as seen on the front and back covers of the *Observer's Handbook* over the years.

Although a retired professional astronomer with an MS from the University of Minnesota, like my colleagues, I have a great appreciation for the observational work done by RASCals and other amateur astronomers, who continue to make significant discoveries of new phenomena and report their observations to the appropriate international scientific associations. This astronomical data has been useful in formulating hypotheses about, for example, the formation of the solar system.

October 18, 2021

3

Infinite Regressions

A recent essay in the science e-zine *Quanta* described "quantum chromodynamics" as a fancy way of referring to the innards of subatomic particles, with their gluons, quarks and antiquarks, and I was reminded of a story by Vladimir Nabokov first published in 1939 in Russian and subsequently translated into English for a 1963 issue of *Esquire*. Titled "The Visit to the Museum," the story is of a visitor who finds himself trapped in an endless progression of rooms with unusual displays, a Borgesian labyrinth of infinite regression, much like those book covers that show a picture of someone holding the very same book, with its cover displaying a picture of someone holding the very same book, with its cover ...

What at first sight seemed to be a true picture of matter turns out to be something more complex, whose parts themselves appear to also be composed of ever smaller parts, a kind of infinite progression not readily visualized at our macro level of vision. Each time a fundamental understanding of structure was achieved, further scientific research revealed yet more fundamental possibilities for division.

In the fifth century BCE the Greek philosopher Democritus described matter as being composed of individual particles he thought were indivisible — atoms. And in the mid-nineteenth century Russian chemist Dmitri Mendeleev devised the periodic table of elements, showing that the elements differed from one another in their atomic weights. Following the later discovery of radioactivity by Marie Curie, in the twentieth century appeared the familiar picture of atoms whose nuclei differed from one another in the amount and kind of subatomic particles — protons and neutrons. Even these subatomic particles themselves were found to be divisible and composed of yet smaller entities called quarks and antiquarks.

Like Mendeleev's periodic table of the elements, particle physicists in the twentieth century devised a table of known atomic particles by classifying them according to their composition of quarks and antiquarks. Called the standard model of particle physics, it classifies all known elementary particles and accounts for three of the four known fundamental forces: electromagnetism, the weak force and the strong force. (It fails to include gravitational force.) The standard model has been successful in the experimental confirmation of quarks with many different particles, both predicted and observed. It has been unsuccessful, however, in including a number of fundamental interactions with general relativity, or in accounting for cosmological phenomena such as the accelerating expansion of the universe and other requirements deduced from astronomic observation, like dark matter and dark energy.

While the standard model may resemble the beginning of an infinite regression, theoretical and experimental particle physicists, as well as cosmologists, continue to work in elucidating our understanding of matter and time, underlying the composition and future of the universe of which we ourselves are but a very small part that just so happens to be conscious.

March 9, 2021

4

Quantum Superpositions

The age-old question, "Which came first, the chicken or the egg?" is a clear example of an enigma of causality. In an updated version of this physics thought experiment, Alice and Bob are in their kitchen. Washing dishes, Alice accidentally drops a plate. The sound startles Bob, who then burns himself on the stove and yells "F——!" Alternatively, first Bob burns himself and cusses, which causes Alice to drop a plate.

At our usual level of existence, somewhere in the middle between the extremely small (to us) domain of atomic particles and the barely conceivable (for us) enormous realms of intergalactic space and time, the temporal relationship of cause and effect compels us to assert that only one of these two versions of the events in Alice and Bob's kitchen is possible. The answer "both" is logically impossible, with this impossibility arising from the one word in the question referencing time: *first*.

Like Schrödinger's cat — alive and dead at the same time — this story of Alice and Bob illustrates the absurd result obtained when quantum mechanics, which elegantly serves the micro world of subatomic particles in its ability to predict experimental outcomes, is used to describe macro phenomena, like chickens and eggs or kitchen chaos.

The problem of Schrödinger's cat, or Alice and Bob's kitchen, is one of logic, of seemingly alternative physics involving cause and effect (i.e., time), one for the micro and another for our macro world. Having banished theology to the realm of the meaningless, it appears that the "scripture" of quantum mechanics requires us to perform a "willing suspension of disbelief," permitting concepts like superposition and entanglement to describe situations we would normally label as either true or false.

Attempts to reconcile the apparent logical contradiction by invoking coherence and decoherence in quantum wave theory make sense, but then again angelic intervention may make sense to a theologian confronted with explaining parthenogenesis. Comparing quantum physics to Christian scripture may sound outlandish, but hey, the ideational structures of each cohere (so to speak).

In his book *Helgoland*, theoretical physicist Carlo Rovelli illustrates the apparent paradox of superposition arising from quantum theory and how it can be resolved by a conceptual shift. A rocky, barren and windswept island in the North Sea, Helgoland (or Heiligenland, meaning "holy land") was visited by the twenty-three-year-old Werner Heisenberg, who, suffering from allergies, sought the island's pollen-free atmosphere from which to concentrate on the difficulty of explaining how an electron can jump from one orbit to another within an atom, and just how that transition occurs. Using the mathematical technique of matrix algebra, Heisenberg successfully accounted for the phenomenon by abandoning the concept of simultaneity in determining both the position and momentum of a particle: one or the other, but not both at the same time, unlike in classical or Newtonian mechanics. This "uncertainty principle" became a major contribution to the understanding of quantum theory.

The logical paradox of quantum superposition, however, has been a stumbling block in understanding quantum theory. Even its creators admitted that some of its interpretations defied reason, as with Schrödinger's cat. Unlike Erwin Schrödinger, Rovelli describes how matter can be thought of as a network of relationships rather than of objects, and the imaginary cat now resumes its existence not by itself, but in relation to other entities, like the box enclosing it or the observer, and therefore it cannot be both alive and dead at the same time.

This trick of disentangling superposition gives credibility to the quantized view of interpreting nature by asking us to alter the way we think about matter itself. Rovelli resolves the paradox of the quantum entanglement of two separated but previously combined objects with the addition of a third one, the observer, who is always present. The apparently impossible contact between the two objects then vanishes and the logical paradox is seen as illusory, as matter is now defined in terms of its relationships. Yet this seems contrary to how we perceive experience, with there being no Kantian *ding an sich* (a thing as it is, in itself).

This would not be the first time our naive understanding of natural phenomena has been challenged. The realization that the sun does not rise at dawn, but rather it is the Earth's rotation that makes it appear so, as well as maintaining that we live on the surface of a rotating spheroid, only vexes the few remaining adherents of flat Earth theory.

May 9, 2021; combined with "The Cat Came Back," June 9, 2021

5

Of Quasars and Faint Blue Stars

Established by Catherine Wolfe Bruce, an American philanthropist and patron of astronomy, the Bruce Medal is an annual award is given by the Astronomical Society of the Pacific to a professional astronomer in recognition of a lifetime of outstanding achievement and contributions to astrophysics research.

First awarded to Simon Newcomb in 1898, the medal has since gone to some of the greatest astronomers of the past century. In 1975 Allan Sandage won the award for having determined the first reasonably accurate values for the Hubble constant, a unit that describes how fast the universe is expanding at different distances from a particular point in space, relevant to determining the age of the universe. Earlier, in 1963, Sandage and fellow scientist Thomas Matthews published a definite identification of a radio source with an optical object. They had detected what appeared to be a faint blue star at the location of the radio source.

Dutch American astronomer Willem Luyten's major contribution to the discipline was the search among faint blue stars for white dwarfs, an end stage of stellar evolution. I studied under Luyten at the University of Minnesota and collaborated with him at the National Observatory of Argentina from 1955 to 1963, later writing my master's thesis, titled "A Search for Quasars Among Faint Blue Stars," under his advisement in 1966. Our findings were published in the *Astrophysical Journal*, and fittingly, as the senior researcher, Luyten was awarded the Bruce Medal in 1968.

Over the following years it was noted that these "quasi-stellar galaxies," as they were first understood, were such a great distance from us they could serve as reference points in constructing models of the rotation of our own galaxy. Later investigations revealed that these intense sources of radiation were associated with massive black holes located in galactic centres. Stephen Hawking then employed quantum physics to finally understand the production of the observed intense radiation emitted at the periphery, or "event horizon," of these objects, thus merging the quantum "micro-" and cosmological "macro-" representations of matter and revealing the origin of what astronomers can observe and measure of these beacons of radiation in the intergalactic darkness, each "burning" in the sky without itself being consumed — a burning bush of the cosmos.

Combining particle physics with astrophysics has been particularly fruitful in terms of learning details of stellar evolution. Data accumulated by orbiting telescopes continues to pour in, and direct reconnaissance with space missions to nearby bodies in the solar system adds to our collective knowledge, each new discovery revealing further problems to solve.

June 9, 2021

6

Astrology

Marketed as a harmless diversion in the miscellaneous amusement pages of newspapers, along with Sudoku and crossword puzzles, personal horoscopes are not ordinarily taken seriously by most. Nevertheless, their assertions and predictions may lurk in the unconscious, providing a possible subjective sense of significance to life events, mundane or otherwise. A quick web search for *horoscopy* reveals, for example, that "Scorpios are controlling because they're suspicious. They like to know everything that's going on, and they don't exactly think the best of things in every situation."

But beyond the manifest silliness of horoscopy, astrology has a distinguished and not-to-be-dismissed relevance to the history of science, arising from the human attribute of *cognoscere*, the seeking of explanations about how things work. In his book *A Scheme of Heaven: Astrology and the Birth of Science*, Alexander Boxer links ancient and medieval astrology to modern data science, assuming, we are told, that while modern horoscopy is "total bullshit," it is nevertheless interesting bullshit, and fun to play around with.

The field of astrology arose from the search for patterns among the mountains of positional data recorded about planetary motion by ancient observers. These data later became useful in constructing a modern heliocentric view of the solar system, first by Nicolaus Copernicus, then by Johannes Kepler, who elucidated the laws of planetary motion, and Galileo, who documented the moons of Jupiter and the rings of Saturn. Finally, and by, in his own words, "standing on the shoulders of giants," Isaac Newton's laws of motion heralded the birth of astronomy, now separated from its astrological predecessor.

Long before the Renaissance, the ancient Greeks knew about planetary movements among the fixed stars and conceived models of cosmic structure to account for what they observed, such as Ptolemy's second-century compendium *Almagest* (which was only made possible by drawing upon many older preclassical observations, such as those made by the Babylonians). While once widely believed, but later disproven by Kepler, Ptolemy's theory, using epicycles to account for retrograde planetary movement, was still the result of *reason*. Even the mythological stories of gods and goddesses running the universe, such as the Greek god of light and the sun, Apollo, with his golden chariot, and Selene, the Greek goddess of the moon, with her moon chariot, were themselves examples of basic human *cognoscere*.

Boxer describes how the two major astrological systems — one based on the "sign" of one's birth and the other on the "house," or the time and location of one's birth — are used to classify the positional locations of celestial objects. In comparison, a working astronomer aiming a telescope would use the more rigorous concepts of declination and right ascension in the apparent celestial sphere, coordinates analogous to latitude and longitude in the terrestrial one.

Not discussed in Boxer's book, however, is the Chinese system of twelve rotating signs to which one is assigned depending on one's year of birth. Compatibility between two people is allegedly predetermined by their individual signs. Noting, however, that data collections lead to interpretation of patterns, Boxer concludes that observers should beware of unwarranted conclusions about causality, for trends in data may not be neutral in their effects on daily living. Explaining this can be frustrating to believers, like a new acquaintance who asked my sign and, when told, walked away muttering, "I can't handle Scorpios ..."

June 29, 2021

7

Music of the Spheres

The ninth studio album of British rock band Coldplay, *Music of the Spheres*, was released on October 15, 2021. With the tagline "everyone is an alien somewhere," the title of the album derives from the prescientific concept in which proportions in the movements of celestial bodies — the sun, moon and planets — were understood as a form of music. Originating in ancient Greece, in the fifth century BCE, this idea arose within the Pythagorean school of thought, whereby the relational positioning of the sun, moon and all planets, moving in circles about a hypothesized "central fire," was associated with musical intervals. While the idea of a central fire was incorrect, the suggestion of a relationship between sounds and movements of celestial objects persisted as an idea until the post-Renaissance scientific revolution in Europe.

The year 2021 also saw the publication of the book *Alien Listening* by music professors David K.L. Chua of the University of Hong Kong and Alexander Rehding of Harvard University. The book was inspired by the 1977 NASA launch of the *Voyager* capsule, the only object created by humans to have left the solar system, which contained, among other objects, a recording of different genres of music, introducing ourselves, as it were, to any possible alien civilization that may eventually find it.

Of course, this may not have been a good idea. In the highly acclaimed Chinese science-fiction trilogy *Alien Listening* (2016), written by Cixin Liu and translated into English by Ken Liu, a secret Chinese military project sends signals into space to establish contact with aliens. Unfortunately, an alien civilization captures the signal and subsequently makes plans to invade Earth. The consequences proceed from there into further entanglements.

Chua and Rehding's book plays on ideas involving cosmology and musical theory, from Pythagoras to particle physics. While at times irritating, with its "cute" references to Hollywood sci-fi cinema, its metaphysical speculations and its persistent inappropriate use of *why* rather than *how* in regard to discussing scientific theories, *Alien Listening* is an erudite and entertaining romp through human endeavour.". Chua and Rehding's formulations have an aura of grandiosity, but then, their vast subject matter itself is grandiose.

To connect music and science, from the ancient discovery of tonal ratios to putative vibrations of strings in theoretical physics after two and a half millennia, leads to a fascinating relationship arising from the history of ideas, as well as a unique title in contemporary rock music.

December 11, 2021

8

Gaia Revisited

In the 1970s chemist James Lovelock and microbiologist Lynn Margulis famously proposed what came to be known as the Gaia principle, or hypothesis, which proposed that "living organisms interact with their inorganic surroundings on earth to form a synergistic and self-regulating, complex system that helps to maintain and perpetuate the conditions for life on the planet." (The purposeful use of the word *Gaia* is in reference to the ancient Greek mythological personification of our planet, first alluded to in the eighth or seventh century BCE by Hesiod, in a poem which describes the genealogy of the gods.)

The Gaia hypothesis was initially criticized for being teleological and contrary to the principles of natural selection, and while it continues to attract criticism, it has not been universally assigned to the dustbin of pseudoscience. In a similar vein, in a 2020 essay published in *Aeon* magazine, Canadian evolutionary biologist W. Ford Doolittle of Dalhousie University proposed a theoretical path consistent with Darwinian natural selection. *Multilevel selection theory* entails life being represented as "a hierarchy of entities nested together like Russian dolls, connected by parent-offspring lineages." This concept is lucidly described and illustrated in the essay with thought experiments, such as conceiving of social systems as entities occupying one rung higher than humanity in an imagined "ladder of life."

In a less "down-to-earth" usage of the name of this deity, Gaia is a space observatory of the European Space Agency, launched in 2013, designed to determine the positions, distances and motions of billions of stars with great precision by direct observation from outside the atmosphere of the Earth, unlike former terrestrial observatories that recorded only individual observations. Having worked for several years in the mid-twentieth century photographing stars with a 1.54 meter (60 inch) reflecting telescope at the Bosque Alegre observatory near Córdoba, Argentina, this is particularly interesting to me. With the Gaia observatory, what once had been the laborious work of collecting astrometric data about individual stellar sources has now become a routine extraterrestrial measurement, such as the distribution of faint blue stars in specific directions relative to the plane of the Milky Way, our galaxy.

Bizarrely, the name Gaia also appears in the domain name gaia.com, which claims to offer "thousands of videos on topics that you'll never find in the mainstream media." These are said to cover a multitude of "new age" areas such as "alternative realities, energy healing, ancient lost technology" and dozens more of that ilk, designed for gullible punters willing to part with their money for instruction about ideas that otherwise can be consigned to the aforementioned dustbin of pseudoscience.

December 20, 2020; revised August 27, 2021

Essay #8 was previously accepted for publication in Sky News, *a periodical circulated among amateur astronomers by the Royal Astronomical Society of Canada (RASC), but with the deletion of the final paragraph on Gaia video streaming services because the editor was fearful that even the mention of the website's existence would lead to readers becoming aware of the availability of this rubbish. Hence, its very existence needed to be concealed. Those RASCals sure seem insecure about the acceptance of rational science among their more innocent members ...*

9

Entropy vs. Entaxy

There are more things in heaven and earth,
Horatio, than are dreamt of in your philosophy.

Hamlet, William Shakespeare

The word *philosophy*, in the sense employed by William Shakespeare and others from his time, persisted until the early nineteenth century, when the word *science* came to replace it in describing experimental works of investigation into natural phenomena. This direct observation of phenomena, together with the recording of experimental data, contributed to our understanding of now familiar forces like gravity and electromagnetism, and permitted construction of the laws of motion governing observed movements of celestial bodies, and later the wave/particle representation of light.

The branch of physics known as thermodynamics addresses the relation between energy and heat and is relevant to both astrophysics and cosmology (both branches of astronomy). Formulated in the nineteenth century by James Prescott Joule and William Thomson, 1st Baron Kelvin, the laws of thermodynamics arose not from philosophical speculation about the nature of heat, but from the search for efficient steam engines. The conservation of energy in the first law, and the concept of entropy in the second, describe the flow of time in only one direction, from organized to disorganized matter, and the increasing dispersion of thermal energy, predicting an end state of equilibrium in which all energy has become inaccessible: the "heat death" of the universe, according to the second law of thermodynamics.

Cosmologist Julian Barbour reminds us in the first chapter of his recent book, *The Janus Point: A New Theory of Time*, that the laws of thermodynamics formulated in the nineteenth century refer to closed systems, that is, molecules boxed in a sealed and impermeable container, as in the cylinders of an engine. But the universe is not a rigid box; rather, it is an expanding, unfolding three-dimensional space over time, unconstrained by rigid boundaries.

As a consequence, what we observe in this expanding universe is not an increase in disorganization but the opposite: an increase in complexity characteristic of the process of evolution, not only of living matter, as seen in the progression of species (unicellular → multicellular → asexual reproduction → sexual reproduction), but also in stellar evolution (i.e., the formation of spiral galaxies condensing from an initial soup of quarks) and even intellectual curiosity itself (progressing, in Western culture, from pre-Socratics to quantum mechanics and now to the unsettling prospect of artificial, non-human, intelligent machines).

This progression does not resemble entropy but rather negative entropy, or entaxy, and the remainder of Barbour's book develops this idea in detail: an alternative cosmology that doesn't predict a heat death but instead a continual growth in complexity, what he calls "the single most important concept in the book."

In an expanding universe of matter, we can identify ourselves as participants in this apparently universal process of increasing complexity, and it is humbling to contemplate the grandeur of the cosmos alongside the utter insignificance of we puny, sentient and flawed human organisms. Endowed with this astonishing and mysterious attribute of consciousness, we have the ability to think "outside the box," come whatever may be the fate of unstable *Homo sapiens,* universal heat death perhaps not being inevitable.

June 18, 2021

10

Humanity: Existence and Extinction

Henry Ernest Gee is a British paleontologist, evolutionary biologist and senior editor of the scientific journal *Nature.* His recently published book *A (Very) Short History of Life on Earth: 4.6 Billion Years in 12 Pithy Chapters* was reviewed in the September 2021 issue of *Literary Review* by Australian entomologist Nigel Andrew, who asked the question "What Will Survive of Us?"

A fair question, given the brief (and temporary) existence of *Homo sapiens,* who are now, as a species, plunging towards a new extinction, the ironic consequence of their progressive destruction of that same natural environment that had once allowed their evolution upon the rumpled surface of this planet.

Astronomical measurements of the expansion rate of the universe place the initial "big bang" singularity, and thus the age of our universe, at around 13.8 billion years ago. Our particular solar system — of sun, planets and assorted leftover rubbish, later condensed by gravitation from interstellar material — formed around 4.6 billion years ago. The oldest evidence of ancient biological activity on Earth is currently found in stromatolites, or stromatoliths, layered sedimentary formations created by photosynthetic cyanobacteria. A major constituent of the fossil records of the first known forms of life on Earth, stromatolites' presence here peaked about 1.25 billion years ago before declining, though some are still around.

Experimentally, researchers at the University of Texas in Austin found that cyanobacteria exposed to localized beams of light moved towards the light, expressing positive phototaxis, thereby increasing their photosynthetic yield, which is necessary for survival. The key word here is *photosynthetic*, for the basic process of life on Earth appears to be the transfer of energy by radiation from the nearby star that is our sun to a physical structure that exhibits growth over time through some process of reproduction. Even organisms in the deep sea, without a life source, are nourished by consuming the remains of others that have descended to their depth. No light, no life.

Over geologic time, through periodic extinctions and prolonged ice ages, different forms of life came and went, from unicellular to multicellular organisms, each adapting to the ambient conditions of stability until, like trilobites (none of which survived the Permian mass extinction event that saw the loss of over 90 percent of all animal species) or the dinosaurs, they became extinct, slowly replaced by others, like mammals, and through evolution, eventually primates.

Only comparatively recently, a mere 200,000 years ago, primates in Africa, exhibiting the early characteristics of *Homo sapiens,* heralded the eventual successful emergence of that particular animal species we call human, whose progressive cognitive abilities have led to its apparent dominant position among other living animal species. But *Homo sapiens* has become a victim of its own success and will itself become extinct in the comparatively near future, perhaps within the next few thousand years.

The end of civilization as we know it, however, is much closer, visible now on the horizon as we continue to destroy our natural environment. Having consciousness and the ability to comprehend both *what we are* and the reality of our current situation, we may in fact be at the apogee of understanding. As I speculated some sixty-seven years ago in an essay I wrote for my bachelor's degree at the University of Minnesota, titled "*Auf dem Wege zur Eigenen Weltanschauung,*" what is man but a very small yet complex chunk of the universe come alive and come conscious?

After we have gone, some form of life on Earth will probably continue on until the dying sun expands and incinerates what is left of the planet. Beyond that astrophysically foreseen end to our solar system, cosmologists like Katie Mack, in her recent book

The End of Everything (2020), can only speculate. Gee bluntly concludes, "We owe it to ourselves, and to our fellow species, to conserve what we have and to make the best of our brief existence."

October 12, 2021

LIFE

11

The Polymath

Assembled by Peter Burke, professor emeritus of cultural history at the University of Cambridge, *The Polymath: A Cultural History from Leonardo da Vinci to Susan Sontag* is an encyclopedic compendium of 500 academic polymaths, men and women noted not only for their intellectual achievements but also for having made significant contributions to multidisciplinary learning over the ages.

While the designation *polymath* has traditionally been given to anyone who is interested in learning about many different things, Burke restricts his collection to those who made notable contributions to different branches of academic inquiry in the centuries since the late Middle Ages. It is not a list of us many relatively unlearned and confessedly ignorant students who simply like to learn about how things work.

Following an introduction of his criteria for inclusion in the volume is a chapter titled "East and West," in which Burke describes the history of polymathy in ancient cultures, including those of Greece, Rome and China, and later the Islamic world and the early and high Middle Ages. Subsequent chapters introduce the cultural milieux of the Renaissance man and, in turn, detail four different ages of polymathy up until the end of the twentieth century: "the Renaissance Man (1400–1600)"; "Monsters of Erudition (1600–1700)"; "The 'Man of Letters' (1700–1850)"; and "Territoriality (1850–2000)." Each chapter contains short biographical sketches of scholars identified in every period as being multidisciplinary in their writings.

In the remaining chapters, Burke goes on to examine the commonality of these scholars, their habitats and values, before describing contemporary interdisciplinary studies at universities and his concerns about how the internet has affected these areas of intellectual interest. Websites like Wikipedia, or other open-source educational sites that make scientific journals publicly available, facilitate information exchange. One may now, for example, make the literary connection between an ancient goddess, Gaia, and a European extraterrestrial observatory. Burke's concerns about the internet, however, seem not to refer to the exchange of scientific information but rather to the wide dissemination of false, or at least provisional, information, such as occurs over social media or websites that promote pseudoscientific beliefs like astrology or many religious doctrines.

I personally was able to identify with much of what Burke describes about polymaths, having spent time in childhood engrossed in encyclopedias, later receiving university degrees in humanities, astronomy, medicine and psychiatry, and working in all these areas until finally, in retirement, indulging my literary whims by penning a series of short essays, though denying any academic pretensions of expertise, with two exceptions (both now out of date with current understanding): professional training in astronomy in the mid-twentieth century and diagnostic expertise in the assessment of mental disorders and their treatment in the late twentieth century. My life has been, in Isaiah Berlin's dichotomy, more foxlike (knowing many things) than that of hedgehoggery (knowing one big thing). I'm not sure if that's a virtue or a vice. Some would call it a "Jack of all trades but a master of none."

January 11, 2021

12

Medical Education

Instruction in the art and science of healing has been historically documented in many diverse human cultures. For example, in the fifth century BCE the Greek historian Herodotus described the specialization of Egyptian physicians in contrast to the prevailing "general practice" approach of the Greeks, as was taught in the classical medical schools at Cos and Knidos and documented in the *Corpus Hippocraticum.*

The summit of ancient Western medical knowledge was attained with the work of surgeon, anatomist and philosopher Galen of Pergamum (129–216 CE), known for his written systemization of what was considered medical knowledge at the time of his writing. His understanding of internal anatomy and medicine was influenced by, but limited to, the then current theory of the four humours: black bile, yellow bile, blood and phlegm. (He never performed a dissection of a human cadaver, instead studying animals to reveal the organs of the body to be found beneath the skin.)

Galen's views of the cause of disease dominated and influenced Western medical science for more than 1,300 years, until Andreas Vesalius published the first realistic account of human anatomy in 1543. Soon thereafter, the older beliefs about the humours succumbed to direct observation through dissection. Vesalius became a professor of anatomy at Padua University in Italy, where he was renowned for being the first to teach with the dissection of cadavers. Though there were older medical schools, dating from the seventh century, in Southern Europe, such as in Salerno, this innovation led to a proliferation of medical teaching.

The practice of opening medical schools attached to universities was first developed in Europe and later spread to North America. The first program of medical education in Canada was created in 1824 at the Montreal Medical Institution, five years later becoming the Faculty of Medicine at McGill University. The standard requirement of medical education in North America was set out in a 1910 report by Abraham Flexner, who stated that "schools of medicine must have high standards for the admission of students, must be part of and subject to the rigorous academic standards of a university, must base their educational programs on a scientific approach to medicine, and must encourage the scholarly research of their faculties."

Contemporary incorporation of pseudoscientific "healing practices" into curricula of medical schools may fail to live up to the standards of the Flexner Report in terms of academic rigour and scholarly approach. It will be interesting to see how this unfolds in the coming stressful years of social collapse.

January 10, 2022

13

Beds and Infrastructure at UBC

As a graduate of the University of British Columbia medical school in 1976, and after training there in psychiatry and joining the faculty, I rose to the position of Clinical Associate Professor of Psychiatry. From my initial admission interview in 1971 to my final receipt of the "Acknowledging Your Contributions" form letter when I departed after twenty-three years, I became familiar with many of the academic and clinical teachers providing instruction about the art and science of medicine throughout this period of time.

In 1994 I left the hothouse scenes of simultaneously heading an acute-care inpatient service and being the consultant in psychiatry with the AIDS Clinical Care Team at St. Paul's Hospital in Vancouver. As the HIV epidemic waned with the development of viral suppressant therapy, I decided to pursue a quieter and cooler retirement in the Yukon Territory, as the only clinical psychiatrist in an area the size of France with a population of about 30,000 souls.

Now fully retired from practice, after half a century, I remain grateful for the outstanding educational experiences received at

UBC. Many of the professors and clinicians I knew personally are mentioned in *Dreamers, Skeptics, and Healers* by Wendy Cairns et al. (1943–2018). Cairns's book is not a book about the treatment of sick people or the pursuit of research in the health sciences, nor is it one about the pedagogy of clinical medicine. It is a book about the history of the infrastructure of an institution in BC designed to facilitate the learning of those skills required to pursue a career as a physician providing medical services, and at the same time to create a multidisciplinary venue for the pursuit of medical science, both of these activities being noble and humane occupations.

Established in 1950, the solid infrastructure of UBC's medical school, the buildings housing the physical resources, today includes the lecture halls, teaching aids, laboratory facilities, resource libraries, faculty and administrative offices, and more. The human infrastructure includes the teaching faculty, biological scientists and administrative officers, these three being the primary focus of Cairns's book. Within its pages are glowing accounts of dozens of individual participants in the formation, growth and expansion of the medical school from a temporary hut for the first 60 students to today's distributive model with four campuses and nearly 300 students in each of the four undergraduate years, with many more in postgraduate programs.

The perseverance of the faculty, along with their frustrations and successes, is carefully presented, often in minute detail, such as the minutes of meetings documenting the lively debates among these gifted and intelligent men and women of both the scientific and clinical faculties, including founding members Constance and Sydney Friedman. All were determined to succeed in creating what they termed a "world-class" facility (though of course also driven by their normal individual desires to advance their careers). These intricate accounts of faculty meetings will doubtless be fascinating reading for those who were involved and still remember their outcomes, but for ordinary readers among today's scientists and clinicians, not to mention the general public, they are about as interesting as the fine details of deuteronomistic genealogy to the average Christian or Jewish non-scholar.

The book is divided into seven chapters, chronologically moving from the initial desire to create a provincial medical school to the first classes held in 1950 and still to the present day (2020), simultaneously describing the growth of physical infrastructure along with brief biographies of those who, over seventy years, contributed to its growth and resources. Little is said about the other two major participants in the enterprise: the students themselves, or the ultimate intended beneficiaries — the patients. The latter word does not even appear in the index, which consists almost entirely of the names of the professors, scientists, administrators, politicians and philanthropic benefactors (whose names, in exchange for cash donations, are prominently displayed on various buildings around the four campuses distributed across BC) who contributed to the emergence of what Cairns refers to as the present "world-class" institution.

Financial issues were the bugbear of the medical school's expansion, once involving monetary considerations concerning apportionment of public vs. private beds in teaching hospitals before the arrival of universal Medicare. (In hospital jargon, *beds* are defined as containers for holding sick, non-ambulatory people unable to be treated as outpatients. The size of a hospital is measured by the number of beds it contains.) British Columbia entered the federal Medicare program on July 1, 1968, and concerns over public vs. private "bed ownership" became moot, though monetary issues for doctors remained. (Some still continue to advocate for private hospitals, where wealthy patients can pay to avoid long waiting lists for non-urgent emergency surgeries.)

The book's focus, then, is primarily about beds, not sick people. It's not a book about medicine or ideas about healthy living. It is not about teaching methods or the treatment of disease. There is only minimal content addressing pedagogic details about what is to be taught, or how it should be taught. It is about the history and infrastructure of an educational institution, its buildings, locations, sites, costs, design, contents and nomenclature. It is also a book about control, careers, responsibility, division of labour and money. It is undeniably self-servingly positive, yet deservedly so, a story of remarkable advances in the provision of medical services to citizens in the province of British Columbia over the past seventy years.

That said, it is nevertheless a beautiful and inspiring book, similar to a coffee table art book, unlikely to be read on the bus on the way to school or work or for bedtime perusal. Never intended to be a bestseller, *Dreamers, Skeptics, and Healers* probably will be found in waiting rooms for patients, where it will hopefully promote positive expectations about their forthcoming medical consultations, diagnoses and treatments.

In any event, the text will surely become a treasured historical document, available to anyone interested in the development of the UBC medical school. It ably delivers what was promised.

Originally published in the *Ormsby Review*, January 29, 2022

14

Scattered Limbs

Recorded as notes for over three decades, *Scattered Limbs*, by physician and writer Iain Bamforth, is a collection of short essays (often a page or two, though at times only a single sentence) expressing a thought or an idea associated with medicine that occurred to the author in moments throughout his career. Subtitled *A Medical Dreambook*, the essays and ideas within the 248-page book are unindexed, and there is no table of contents. Not intended to be read sequentially but to be dipped into as one desires, it is a wondrous treasure chest of ideas that one can mine at random, finding unexpected associations from ancient to modern literature (from Asclepius and Petronius to Kafka and Adorno, and just about everybody in between) in writing about what we might call medicine and humanity.

In the book's short preface, Bamforth writes that his collection "is intended for general readers intrigued by the cultural aspects of medicine." With few anecdotes arising from his work with patients, the collection is not a personal memoir but more like a visit to an imaginary museum of ideas and thoughts relating to health and sickness, expressed by a multitude of writers and thinkers of all kinds — poets, scientists, artists, essayists, etc. — who have all commented on issues of health and illness from their different backgrounds and points of view.

This collection of miscellaneous thoughts and ideas about medicine and life reveals Bamforth to be a thinker whose world view extends well beyond the concerns of science and medical practice, with a broad understanding of issues pertaining to society at large: in essence, the world view of a polymath. On the back cover is a single pithy and relevant quotation from the early eighteenth-century German polymath Gottfried Wilhelm Leibniz: "May it please God that it should come about that doctors philosophize, and philosophers occupy themselves with medicine."

The charm of *Scattered Limbs* lies in the discovery of connections, ideas and relationships often previously unknown to the reader. It illuminates our endless search for understanding life, death and hope, and is akin to philosophy as this subject was understood in the time of the Enlightenment, in the eighteenth century: a discussion of ideas by educated thinkers, unlike modern academic philosophers, who are concerned with linguistic analysis and elaboration of the "true essence of meaning."

The deliberate absence of an index allows readers the challenge and opportunity of making notes for themselves when discovering new nuggets of old wisdom that reveal unexpected connections and throw new light upon eternal mysteries. Essayist Alberto Manguel praises Bamforth's unusual collection as "an antidote to the gloom and doom of our time, meriting inclusion on the shelves of all those interested in the history of ideas."

April 2, 2021

15

All Things, Not Creatures

In her splendid recent review in the *New York Review of Books* of current thinking among natural scientists, ranging from the minute quanta of subatomic particles to the immensity of cosmological speculation about the fate of the universe, Yale professor of astronomy and physics Priyamvada Natarajan examines three books for our curious minds. The clever title of the review, "All Things Great and Small," is particularly apt, since the three volumes discussed address everything that we can currently deduce from our conscious experience of nature, avoiding any hint or reference to a creator or supernatural entity.

Lifted from the title *All Creatures Great and Small*, a popular book and television series about a 1930s Yorkshire veterinarian, the title of Natarajan's review illustrates that familiar ploy of a small subset of writers who specialize in quotes and constructing short and sometimes witty phrases that entice potential readers to not only turn the page but to actually read the content that follows.

The three books under discussion are *Neutron Stars: The Quest to Understand the Zombies of the Universe* by Katia Moskvitch, *The End of Everything (Astrophysically Speaking)* by Katie Mack, and *Fundamentals: Ten Keys to Reality* by Frank Wilczek, all of which may sound like a mouthful of inaccessible erudition but are essentially science journalism at its finest, making accessible to the general public in plain words the concerns of theoretical physicists and astronomers who continue to ask those three fundamental questions posed by Paul Gauguin in 1897: Where do we come from? Who are we? Where are we going?

No mere 500-word blog–essay, such as the one here, can hope to do more than inspire a curious reader to further pursue an understanding of the ideas discussed in Natarajan's review or in the trio of authors' books, but hopefully the clever headline will entice some to buy these books, read them and, as living and sentient beings (not creatures!), stop and enjoy the view.

July 24, 2021

16

Niche Construction

Kevin Laland, a professor of behavioural and evolutionary biology at the University of St. Andrews, has researched and written for decades about how organisms shape and influence their evolutionary environment. All species of living creatures, including humans, appear to modify their surroundings in ways that favour their ability to survive and reproduce.

This phenomenon, called niche construction, differs in principle from the simple Darwinian concept of survival of the fittest in that it accounts for more than just random genomic mutations and a blind response to the environment in the survival and reproduction of organisms, facilitating the success of the species. For example, earthworms adapt to their environment by molding the soil in which they dwell, through tunnelling and burrowing, and by secreting mucus and molting; beavers construct dams to create ponds and shelters; and humans burn and clear forests, presumably to promote and/or increase agricultural activity, supplying food for an expanding population.

While the evolutionary success of a species may be increased by niche construction, there is an environmental price to pay for the increase of reproductive success, for the very actions facilitating survival and reproduction may exhaust the ability of the environment to provide an adequate supply of energy. In the case of human action, this has led to a constriction of resources and global warming. An uncontrolled and unsustainable positive feedback mechanism, an erosion of the former balance of nature, will have dire consequences for the survival of human civilization and other species as we know it.

Laland objectively concludes that "at a time when human niche construction and ecological inheritance are ravaging the planet's ecology and driving a human population explosion, understanding how organisms retool ecology for their own purposes has never been more pressing."

February 8, 2021

17

The Aliens among Us

Speculation about an alien life form insinuating itself into our world is an enduring trope of science-fiction and horror cinema, but in a lengthy review in the May 20, 2021, edition of the *London Review of Books*, Francis Gooding discusses Merlin Sheldrake's *Entangled Life: How Fungi Make Our Worlds, Change Our Minds, and Shape Our Future*, an astonishing revelation of our human fear of another life form among us, whose behaviour seems to share some characteristics we thought were unique to *Homo sapiens*, suggesting that cognitive processes in the absence of a brain may not be just fictional, but realistic.

Not only living among us today, fungi have also been present and reproducing since the early days of our planet, billions of years ago, as evidenced by fossilized traces in ancient rocks. More than just the "flower" of a spore-releasing mushroom, fungus is the proliferating web of mycelium, a network of microscopic threads called hyphae. This web is found everywhere in the world and seems to be neither plant nor animal, instead displaying some features of both. Like neurons, the hyphae use electric signals to transmit information and to control reproductive behaviour, i.e., the dissemination of spores. As Sheldrake writes, "The fungus mycelium does not have a body, instead entering and possessing something else's ... but is a continuous mesh that envelops the earth."

Fungus has a directional memory that it uses to locate and communicate knowledge of food sources, and the ability to adapt itself physically to its surroundings (whether moist or dry, hot or cold), including a wide range of pH tolerance (ambient level of acidity). Some fungal spores have even been shown to survive extraterrestrial conditions in outer space, leading one to think of panspermia, the theory that the seeding of life on Earth began with spores brought to our planet from elsewhere. While this conjecture could conceivably account for the origin of life on an originally lifeless Earth, it is only a notch in the search for the primary origin of *all* living creatures, ultimately only knocking the question of this origin back to an earlier locale.

Extending this concept of non-human, goal-oriented activity into the realm of science fiction, the writings of Polish author Stanisłav Lem feature bizarre plots involving non-human beings on distant planets, including one in which the planet itself is the living organism, whose "skin" is wounded with the landing of a spaceship.

Back on Earth, humans consume some fungi for nutrition but also ingest mushrooms containing psilocybin, a compound that, like lysergic acid (derived from ergot, a fungus that grows on grains), has the "psychedelic" effect of altering brain networks by enhancing connectivity. Producing what has been described as quasi-spiritual feelings, perhaps with an epiphany akin to "awareness of the wholeness of nature," etc., psilocybin may at times be beneficial to some, though not always, nor with all users.

More research is warranted to understand how else humans and fungi interact, and since these organisms and their mysterious network of mycelium have preceded us here on Earth, then perhaps to them, *we* are the aliens.

June 16, 2021

18

Pandemics and Society

On August 11, 2021, the short essay "Plagues and Classical History — What the Humanities Will Tell Us about COVID in Years to Come" was published in *The Conversation* (UK) by Christopher Smith, a professor at the University of St. Andrews. In his essay, Smith describes the relationships among the social construction of illness and health, the biology of disease and the interaction of science and politics. Relevant to us all, and though not reassuring, the essay is rather meaningful. As a natural phenomenon of competition between life forms, both viral and bacterial pandemics always have winnowed the human species.

A classicist specializing in ancient Rome, Smith is knowledgeable about pandemics in antiquity. In Athens, the plague of the fifth century BCE was described in detail by the historian and general Thucydides (460–400 BCE), who wrote, "I will say what it was like in its course and describe here, as one who had the plague myself and saw others suffering from it myself, the symptoms by which anyone who studies it cannot possibly fail to recognize it …" Of this time period, Smith notes that

> This was the generation that would produce the
> most radical questioning of the role and nature of
> the gods, of what we know of the world and how
> we should live. But it also led to a renewed sense
> of militarism and eventual catastrophe: Athens'
> defeat by Sparta and the loss of her empire.

The temptation may be to say that pandemics change everything, but as the ancient author of Ecclesiastes wrote, "There is nothing new under the sun." The Byzantine historian Procopius (500–570 CE), who survived the onset of plague in the sixth century, was also aware of this, and as the court historian of the Byzantine emperor Justinian, documented everything in his preserved *History of the*

Wars, Book II.22. Once again, notes Smith, "everyone became very religious for a while, but then as soon as they felt they were free, they went back to old behaviour. The plague was a wonderful symbol of systemic decline, but people adjust."

It is difficult to imagine that the present post-pandemic future will somehow permit humans worldwide to "adjust" and return to their pre-pandemic state of existence. The pursuit of profit by commercial enterprises will ensure that constraints such as social distancing and the wearing of face masks will be relaxed over time, but increasing population pressure, resulting from forced migrations and from economic and social inequality, will undoubtedly continue to recreate the conditions favouring aerosol transmission of new viral pathogens.

At the individual level, one's sense of safety can be expected to erode. Even now, as the pandemic wanes among the rich and powerful (both states and people), we can document how COVID is becoming endemic in less fortunate jurisdictions. While there may be a superficial sense of returning to a previous normality for some, failure to eliminate the virus and its variants worldwide will guarantee continued outbreaks for others, exacerbated by crowding and climate change. At the group level, in response to deteriorating lifestyles, we can expect to see undesirable social consequences. Conflict and warfare will be inevitable as nations rush to scapegoat one another. This will be the new "normal."

What Smith doesn't elaborate in his essay is the association of the pandemic with the underlying failure of humans to recognize the myth of "progress," in reality a time bomb leading to social collapse, facilitated by global warming. It is a fact of life that organisms compete with others to survive and reproduce. This is the basis of conflicts between medical science (vaccines, sanitation, social distancing, etc.) and agents of infectious disease (i.e., bacteria, viruses). The goals of medical treatment are not only to improve the quality of life but also to avoid death at all costs: lower infant mortality, aid in the recovery of the injured, ameliorate disability for the chronically impaired, defer death for the aged. These truisms do not imply an ethical judgment about what should or should not be done; they are only a statement of how medical science itself contributes to increasing life expectancy and consequent population explosion.

The fundamental cause of the decline, and eventual fall, of human civilization remains, however, that of evolutionary niche modification of the environment by *Homo sapiens*, facilitated by invention and incessant greed, primarily by those already in power. For example, we create environments and opportunities that facilitate crowding and the consequent sharing of respiratory viruses, like cruise ships, mass aviation tourism, sporting events, concerts, gyms and indoor exercise venues, etc. It appears that economic determinism with the pursuit of private profit is the bedrock of some infectious disease.

Pandemics will recur, and environmental degradation by humans will only exacerbate their severity. Some human activities promote life, some don't. This is not rocket science or quantum mechanics.

August 12, 2021; revised November 11, 2021

19

Proust and Epidemiology

A distinguished French specialist in infectious disease, Adrien Proust (1834–1903) was a pioneer epidemiologist, remembered today for his early work in national and foreign programs for the control of bacterial epidemics such as cholera and plague. Trained in Paris and receiving his doctorate in 1862, his early interest in the control of infectious disease brought him renown and academic success, and he later published scientific papers on epidemiology and public health.

Also interested in neurology, Proust wrote a thesis for his doctorate on the different forms of the "softening of the brain," with a title that reflected the then limited understanding of this specialty, and later coauthored a treatise on what is now known as chronic fatigue syndrome with neurologist Gilbert Ballet in 1900. It was later translated into English and published as "The Treatment of Neurasthenia" in 1903.

Becoming a professor in the Faculty of Medicine at the Université de Paris, Proust rose to the post of chief physician at the Hôtel-Dieu de Paris, one of the main clinical sites in Western Europe, and travelled extensively to Germany, Russia and the Middle East for cholera research. He was also a member of the Comité d'Hygiène publique de France and the Académie de Médecine (from 1879), serving as its secretary from 1883 to 1888. Recognized for his achievements worldwide, he is even referenced in the 1985 novel *Love in the Time of Cholera* by Gabriel García Márquez.

Proust was married with two sons, but only one, Robert, followed in his footsteps and pursued a career in medicine. Robert became an eminent and innovative French surgeon, who achieved recognition largely as a gynecologist, though he was also an accomplished urologist, general surgeon and author of a textbook that was very successful in his lifetime, running to six editions. Proust's other son, Marcel, took a very different path, as an author, and wrote a very long novel about the effect on memory of French cuisine.

October 13, 2021

20

Plague Years

Family physician Ross Slotten recently published a moving memoir titled *Plague Years: A Doctor's Journey through the AIDS Crisis*, about caring for AIDS patients in Chicago throughout the HIV epidemic among the gay male population in the 1980s and beyond. It is a convincing account of his dedication to treating an incurable sexually transmitted viral infection as it decimated this devalued minority throughout the US and other countries for a decade before the development of triple suppression therapy in the early 1990s, which suppressed infection but did not eliminate the retroviral agent. Like diabetes, HIV infection then became a chronic rather than an acute illness, requiring lifelong daily medication.

Slotten's memoir describes in detail the trajectory of illness among many of his patients, including friends, lovers and colleagues, as well as his own initial fears of having contracted the illness. Not limiting the work to an account of his hospital and office practice, Slotten also relates political struggles within the gay community and discusses his attendance at international conferences of sub-specialists, as well as a visit to Namibia to familiarize himself with the problems arising from the epidemic on the African continent.

Plague Years is an accurate and well-written summary of the vicissitudes of caring for patients with incurable illness as a primary care physician. It resonates with my own experiences during those years, which overlap somewhat with Slotten's, although I only worked as a consulting psychiatrist in a hospital setting with referred patients, unlike a family doctor, who provides personal care throughout the course of a fatal illness.

Being one step removed from providing individual care to patients granted me some insulation from emotional distress, but I was close enough to appreciate the difficulty of maintaining the necessary medical objectivity when confronted with an unrelenting succession of tragedies among those mostly young men who contracted this progressive and incurable fatal illness.

January 5, 2021

21

Vaccines and Ignorance

As a medical student a half century ago in the early 1970s, I was absorbed in the study of microbiology and the prevention of infectious diseases. During the summer between my first and second year, I worked as an assistant to the public health inspection service in my rural community Nelson, in the West Kootenays of southeastern British Columbia. And later, during my third year, I started an STD (sexually transmitted disease) screening clinic in Vancouver, and seriously considered pursuing a career in public health following graduation. Although I eventually settled on the practice of psychiatry, with the advent of AIDS in the early 1980s, I became involved in the care of patients with this illness (specifically in relation to the neuropsychiatry of HIV disease), reconnecting with my earlier interest in public health.

In antiquity, infectious disease was thought to be some type of punishment by a pagan — or later, Christian — deity, as retribution for the sins of mankind. Infectious agents themselves were unknown until the discovery of bacteria by Antoni van Leeuwenhoek in 1676. Following the pioneering work of Edward Jenner in treating smallpox and in vaccine development, the first modern public health institutions were created in the 1840s, and since then, life expectancy has about doubled worldwide thanks to the control of infectious disease by both sanitation measures and immunization.

Immunization currently prevents two to three million deaths every year from diseases like diphtheria, tetanus, pertussis, influenza and measles, and since the mid-twentieth century, poliomyelitis, which my wife contracted before a vaccine became available, leaving her with a deformed spine and a shortened life. We now have vaccines to prevent more than twenty-one life-threatening diseases. The latest success story has been the rapid development and deployment of vaccines against the novel COVID-19 respiratory virus in the current pandemic.

Immunization is a key component of primary health care and considered to be an essential human right. The popular and false claim that childhood vaccination is associated with autism has been consistently refuted, and a retrospective study of over 500,000 children found no increased risk of developing symptoms of autism in the months following vaccination. While the diagnosis of autism has increased roughly sevenfold from 1988 to 1999, the vaccination rate has remained relatively stable, at about 95 percent.

Opposition to vaccination is tantamount to denying support for the public health goals of diminishing disease, disability and avoidable sickness and death. To remain unvaccinated is not only ignorant but cruel, a display of apathy in the face of increased human suffering and responsibility to one's fellow humans.

But there is nothing to be ashamed of in admitting ignorance, for we are all ignorant of absolutely everything at birth. It is only through science and education that are we able to attain an understanding of the world that we are compelled to share with one another.

March 13, 2021

22

Sex Workers and Public Heath

An obituary in the July 15, 2021, *Lancet* celebrates the life of Indian physician Smarajit Jana, who died of COVID-19 in Kolkata at the age of sixty-eight. He was memorialized by Sushena Reza-Paul, assistant professor in community health services at the University of Manitoba.

A teacher of occupational health and epidemiology, in 1992 Jana began to reframe sex work as work, looking at it from a worker's-rights perspective, with HIV as an occupational hazard. Trusted by the sex workers in his community, Jana interviewed them about the power structures governing their lives and promoted their collective responses, which led to the formation of a committee and subsequently a collective of now 65,000 sex workers in West Bengal, demonstrating how communities can organize themselves and advocate for their own health and welfare.

Beyond counselling and the distribution of condoms, Jana found that the most effective approach to infection control was when the sex workers themselves were participants in decisions over their lives. He recognized that each individual was a necessary component in the life of their community and worthy of the respect and assistance deemed appropriate to all. Thanks to the involvement of Jana, HIV seroprevalence never rose above 10 percent in this community in the late years of the twentieth century.

Jana's pioneering work was praised by the former director of the National AIDS Control Organization in India, and later in Bangladesh, where Jana helped expand HIV prevention strategies among sex workers, injection drug users and truck drivers, whose occupations rendered them potential spreaders of infection among different population centres.

Besides his teaching, Jana was active in national and international advisory positions and continued his promotion of advocacy among those at risk for HIV infection by virtue of their occupation. This compassionate physician was dedicated to working among minorities and others who may have otherwise been devalued as human beings. He has been recognized worldwide by activists for his contribution to public health, who mourn his loss to now another infectious disease.

July 16, 2021

23

"Wellness" and Avoidance

There is an office building in my neighbourhood that advertises itself as a "wellness centre," and features a variety of self-described "specialists," including naturopathic practitioners, massage therapists, chiropractors and dentists who perform tooth whitening services — but no medical doctors.

In his recent collection of musings on medicine and society, *Scattered Limbs*, English physician Iain Bamforth astutely wrote: "Health isn't enough. Now we have wellness and its promise of radiance and effulgence: wellness is the look of health." In other words, the goal of these "wellness" establishments is merely the *appearance* of being healthy.

In 2018 the "wellness economy" was valued at more than $4 trillion, according to figures from the Global Wellness Institute (GWI). The sanitized mission statement of the GWI states: "The Global Wellness Institute™ is a nonprofit organization with a mission to empower wellness worldwide by educating public and private sectors about preventative health and wellness." Although it describes itself as non-profit, the trademark (signalled by the inclusion of a superscript TM in their business's name) suggests a real goal of financial gain. Accordingly, the GWI's website pulls no punches in promotional descriptions like "the top 20 International Markets for Wellness Real Estate" or in announcing itself as "the authoritative source for research on the ($4.5 trillion) global wellness economy, and the go-to resource for businesses, policymakers and academics. It's the only organization that produces market data and deep analysis for all 11 wellness market sectors."

An article about the GWI from the global media company Forbes emphasizes the non-profit's profit and growth within the market. This is hardly surprising, since greed has historically always been part of the human enterprise and denounced by those in every era, from Job to St. Paul in the Bible to King Midas, Karl Marx, Greta Thunberg and so on. It is therefore not surprising that greed continues to be facilitated today by the capitalist neoliberal structure of the world economy.

In the soothing, greenwashing language used by those promoting operations in non-renewable enterprises, like the Alberta tar sands, or providers of "alternative health care" and "wellness," these businesses avoid any reference to unpalatable issues like sickness and death. When privately owned and operated, the primary goal of "wellness centres" is that of maximizing profits — the reference to health and compassion in their advertising is designed to promote sales and maximize profits.

Governmental provision of services may be opposed to private enterprise, but governmental infrastructure is dependent on taxation, and any tax increase is powerfully resisted in democratic societies by conservative political parties who are concerned with promoting private profit. Authorities continue to manipulate language to avoid referring to sickness and death and invest in state-of-the-art modern patient-care facilities; meanwhile the small, local palliative care units remain squirrelled away under the roofs of old buildings, shamefully dependent on donations and bequests despite providing compassionate care to those in the final stages of their lives.

Most appropriately, my friendly neighbourhood "wellness centre" is located just down the street from the manufacturer and purveyor of tombstones and graveyard monuments, itself conveniently situated around the corner from a large cemetery, both unspoken reminders of our human mortality.

June 23, 2021

MIND

24

The Scientific Method

Henry M. Cowles's recent contribution to the history and philosophy of science, *The Scientific Method*, was reviewed in the January 1, 2021, edition of the *Times Literary Supplement* by British Australian philosopher and historian of science Stephen Gaukroger. Cowles's work, subtitled *An Evolution of Thinking from Darwin to Dewey*, examines the mind itself as an object of scientific inquiry.

After describing the rise of the "scientific method" in the early nineteenth century, which combined the observation of physical phenomena with experimental evidence that could be replicated by other independent investigators to verify hypotheses, Cowles addresses the subsequent rise of scientific psychology, which came to replace previous "speculative accounts of the mind," like psychoanalysis. Building upon Darwin's theory of evolution, the later work of John Dewey led to an experimental approach to psychology grounded in empiricism. Dewey shifted the focus of his research from what we *observe* to how we *think*, expanding the previously held notion of science as a method in which behaviour was the only legitimate object of a true science of psychology.

After Dewey, returning to physical measuring, experimental anthropometric mental testing, such as the intelligence quotient (IQ) test, was employed by Raymond Cattell in his studies of recent immigrants to the US in the early twentieth century to assess educational needs and employment suitability. This early work, though now seen as shallow, led to more sophisticated approaches to testing, celebrated as "scientific" by later psychologists.

Unlike the "hard sciences," like physics or biology, the "science of the mind," other than perhaps the medical and neurological approach to the study of the brain, is sometimes tainted by questionable results, even those allegedly deemed "scientific," obtained by experimental, empirical testing. In 2015, efforts by an international team of university-based researchers to replicate the reported results of previously published studies illustrated the often dodgy results from psychological experiments as reported in major psychological journals. Repeating the procedures of published experiments as detailed, the team's replication of the results failed overall about two-thirds of the time, for experiments in both the social and cognitive subspecialties.

This is one reason that psychology should not be considered a hard science, in which experimental findings can be consistently replicated by other investigators. As Gaukroger notes, "This is not just a problem for psychology, but more generally for the idea of a scientific method that is taken to guarantee objective results." Cowles's book, examining how the connections between the scientific method and psychology came to be accepted, is praised as a welcome discussion of this issue in the philosophy of science.

The implications for medical research, particularly in psychiatry, are obvious, as when formulaic algorithms are used to assign diagnoses without directly interviewing the patient, possibly leading to inappropriate pharmaceutical interventions. When I ran a hospital psychiatric ward, I gave up asking for opinions from the staff psychologist, whose approach was limited to having the patient complete a questionnaire, like a personality inventory, which always led to an unhelpful report of "People who score _____ are more likely to be _____." An intern might stop there and order medications, but I always insisted on a direct interview with the patient before undertaking any intervention.

In 1992, I recall being told by a Russian psychoanalyst in Moscow, whose traditional Freudian approach to mental illness was now once again permitted after the collapse of the USSR, that he was relieved to finally engage in "scientific" treatments with his patients. Bemused, I could only comment that it must be agreeable to have such a positive opinion about one's work.

January 1, 2021

25

Proust and Science

Marcel, son of the distinguished epidemiologist Adrien Proust and brother of the renowned surgeon Robert Proust, had no dream of becoming a medical specialist. His goal was literary, not scientific, and after following a series of minor attempts at fiction, he wrote his final masterpiece about time, memory and its recovery when jolted by a familiar sensation, such as the taste of a biscuit, a tune or a proprioception when walking on uneven flagstones. *In Search of Lost Time* burst over the traditional writing of the era like a brilliant butterfly emerging from its chrysalis, heralding a new approach to fiction. Proust modelled his protagonist after himself, a harbinger of change, perhaps psychologically akin but totally unalike in style to that of his contemporary James Joyce and the equally influential work *Ulysses*.

While many millions of words dealing with literary and textual analysis of Proust's prose have been and continue to be written about his vast creation, his influence on scientific thought at the time should also be acknowledged, for Proust was familiar with a range of cultural matters, not limited to only those of French literature.

Thibault Damour, permanent professor at the Institut des Hautes Études Scientifiques, compared Proust's description of the dimension of time with the works of Albert Einstein, for Proust's gigantic novel displays multiple references to time as a dimension, both as experienced subjectively and as a duration. Both the novelist and the physicist regarded our subjective sense of the flow of time as an illusion. Editor-in-chief of *Physics Today* Charles Day, in describing Proust's narrator reflecting on an ancient church and its accoutrements as different in quality from its milieu, observes how the building persists in the four dimensions of space-time, the fourth being time itself, surrounded by other structures that come and go.

Interpreters have analyzed Proust's novel in every possible way, from self-help, as in the amusing but trivial *How Proust Can Change Your Life* (1997) by Alain de Botton, to the more reflective *Proustian Uncertainties* (2020) by Saul Friedländer, which reflects on how Proust dealt with difficult issues like Jewishness and same-sex desire in light of the prevailing cultural values at the time of the novel's first publication.

In addition to his relativistic and scientific world view, Proust shared with Sigmund Freud (whom he never met) an interest in the new concept of unconscious motivations of human behaviour, though they differed in their understanding of its effects on personality. Freud's psychoanalysis claimed to change the unknown into the known, relieving one of the suppressed conflicts that induce distressing symptoms, whereas Proust compared the sudden recognition of an event to the awakening of forgotten memories, a renewal of awareness. The memories themselves, having remained in the unconscious, are only accessible when jolted by a physical sensation associated with the moment of the event's first appearance, such as a taste, an odour or a touch.

Well educated and no stranger to psychology or physical science, Proust also sagely observed that the understanding of how celestial bodies function (astrophysics) must be easier to comprehend than the sources of human behaviour. As someone trained in both astronomy and psychiatry, this makes sense to me.

And then there's the delicious prose. At last finished with the novel after spending a full year — ten minutes at a time, several times daily, while exercising on a stationary bike — reading the 1,267,069 words in the superb English translation by C.K. Scott Moncrieff from beginning to end, I considered starting over again (this time in French), like an English Proustophile I once knew in Argentina.

Though I probably won't. Other foreign literary sirens are calling, like Thomas Mann (in German) and Miguel de Cervantes (in Spanish).

October 15, 2021

26

Physics and Philosophy

The French author Michel Houellebecq (originally named Michel Thomas, he later changed his surname to that of his communist grandmother) was the winner of the prestigious Prix Goncourt literary prize in 2010. Several years later, Houellebecq wrote a brief autobiographical essay titled "En présence de Schopenhauer," which described his epiphany upon discovering Arthur Schopenhauer's philosophical writings while in his late twenties. After reading a review of the English translation by Andrew Brown in the *New York Review of Books*, I bought the short book of essays. Having read Houellebecq's earlier novels *Submission* (2015) and *Serotonin* (2019), I wondered what he had to say about this old German philosopher who wrote over 200 years ago.

In the early years of the eighteenth century, a young Schopenhauer felt he lacked the interest to follow in the footsteps of his successful merchant father, and being curious about science and philosophy, for a time worked with the German writer Johann Wolfgang von Goethe in his unsuccessful investigations into optics and colour. At university, Schopenhauer spent more time and intellectual energy attending lectures on science than those on philosophy, though he was nonetheless influenced by Immanuel Kant's writings about reason.

Upon its publication, Schopenhauer's monumental work *The World as Will and Representation* (1818) slowly gained academic acclaim, and his philosophy has since inspired scientists like Albert Einstein and Erwin Schrödinger, as well as others who thought about the world and the human condition as having no purpose or inner nature other than a blind striving to survive and reproduce. Schopenhauer subsequently became known as the paramount philosopher of pessimism, though he viewed himself as a realist.

While I generally knew who Schopenhauer was, what he wrote about and his reputation for pessimism, I had never read about him in much detail until picking up Houellebecq's recent essay, which revealed his own initial sense of wonder upon discovering the ideas of the great philosopher, particularly regarding Schopenhauer's concept of *will* as accounting for both gravitational fields in physics and for an organism's drive to survive and reproduce in biology. Like Schopenhauer, I was not enthused about a career in business when I was at university in the mid-1950s, and though I took courses in both philosophy and science, unlike Schopenhauer, I eventually opted for careers in first astronomy then medicine, yet always retaining an interest in philosophical ideas, particularly in science.

Reading Houellebecq's essay abruptly produced my own epiphany, relating my *Weltanschauung* to those of both Schopenhauer and Houellebecq, an unexpected connection illuminating an underlying similarity between physics and biology. Thanks "Mike Wellbeck," for bringing this to my attention, for you have clarified a fundamental relationship subsuming physics, biology and philosophy, making even black holes sound sexy.

May 30, 2021

27

Is Philosophy an Art?

Is philosophy an art? Philosophically speaking, I suppose that depends on what is meant by each of the two nouns in this question, which was recently posed in a critical review in the *New York Review of Books* by the British savant John Gray, whose recent book *Feline Philosophy* addresses the benefits of living in the moment, much like a cat, not worrying about mortality. An often sensible approach for those with end-of-life issues.

Gray poses the question in his review of the book *Witcraft: The Invention of Philosophy in English* by Jonathan Rée, who discounts the idea of philosophy as a continuum of abstract thought from the pre-Socratics to the present day, and instead suggests that individual writers and practitioners of philosophy are best considered as artists whose media are not visual or aural but rather abstract (an idea that might also be assigned to practitioners of the art of pure mathematics).

Ideational conflict between philosophers is evident from the earliest (Western) times, and in his review Gray alludes to the twentieth-century Austrian philosopher Ludwig Wittgenstein, who somewhat enigmatically observed that he found logic and philosophy to be "nonsense, but nonsense of a significant kind." (Gray's review is accompanied by the reproduction of an image of Wittgenstein's fierce and determined-looking face staring fixedly at the viewer before a Mondrianesque background.)

Rée's history of philosophy limits itself to English post-medieval history, but within its constraints of time and language, Gray has found in Rée's book "a rich account of anglophone philosophy during the period discussed." But Rée's rejection of philosophy as a continuum of enquiry into issues associated with the human condition, to any extent, limits *Witcraft*, à la Jorge Luis Borges, "to resemble a folly, full of unexpected doors and labyrinthine passageways, leading nowhere."

Reading Gray's review provoked me to consider to what extent I consider myself a philosopher, and I must confess that although interested in philosophical issues, often expressing this interest in what I read and write, my art or literary craft is neither new nor original, and for that reason I do not claim expertise in philosophy or other intellectual activities. Being resigned to the identity of journalist, reporting to possibly interested readers on what personally seems significant, philosophically or otherwise, I regard myself as a purveyor of entertainment, not of wisdom.

April 29, 2021

28

The Murder of Professor Schlick

The lurid title of David Edmonds's book *The Murder of Professor Schlick* was clearly a marketing decision by the usually sedate Princeton University Press, apparently an attempt to lure devotees of the murder mystery genre to shell out for an academic thriller. But it is nothing of the sort. Rather, it is a detailed historical account of a group of European philosophers who founded logical empiricism as a major academic movement in the twentieth century, establishing the philosophy of science as we know it today. This is clarified somewhat in the book's subtitle, *The Rise and Fall of the Vienna Circle*.

In the 1920s, the Vienna Circle arose out of a discussion group focusing on the writings of Bertrand Russell and Ludwig Wittgenstein. The members considered metaphysics to be meaningless, and the primary role of philosophy to be the support of natural science. With the rise of Adolf Hitler's fascism in neighbouring Germany and endemic anti-Semitism in Austria, in the 1930s the Vienna Circle's members began to disperse, mostly to the UK and the US, where they became part of the academic mainstream, publishing papers in the international journal of the philosophy of science they founded, *Erkenntnis,* which continues to be printed today.

On June 22, 1936, the convener of the Vienna Circle, Moritz Schlick, was shot dead by a deranged former student at the University of Vienna. The assassin was immediately apprehended, tried, found guilty and sentenced to ten years, "with his conditions to be aggravated four times a year by having to sleep on a hard bed." A tragic end indeed for the esteemed scholar, but no mystery, as the title of Edmonds's book would imply, for it is covered in great detail in chapter fifteen.

Another member of the Vienna Circle, Herbert Feigl, joined the philosophy department at the University of Minnesota in 1940, where he continued to meet periodically with other former members who had also emigrated to the US. It was my good fortune as an undergraduate humanities student to have Feigl as one of my professors. Having first trained as a scientist in chemistry, his approach to the philosophy of science reflected his initial grounding in observation, to be done before theorizing about results. This came to be how I myself felt about first doing observational astronomy and gathering data before then analyzing and deriving conclusions about what was observed.

Feigl and I later became friends and spent time listening to classical music together, both of us admirers of the Austrian composer Anton Bruckner and his majestic symphonic creations.

February 15, 2021

29

What's the Point?

The answer to the question "What's the point?" reflects the context in which it is posed, such as the emphasis on *opinion* in law or debate as something upon which to assign a cause or base a conclusion. But for a scientist or mathematician, a point is regarded as a location in four-dimensional space-time specifying a *where* and a *when*, the former being expressed by three spatial coordinates and the latter by one temporal.

Any event may thus be located in four-dimensional space-time by four numbers, conventionally designated x, y, z and t. For example, I wrote this essay in a room located at a specific latitude and longitude (x and y), at an elevation of a certain distance above sea level (z), at a specific time of day within an established time zone, and on a particular day and year in the Gregorian calendar (t). This description of a point works well enough at the local, or macro, level of everyday life, but it is inadequate at both the micro level of particle physics and the mega level of cosmology.

The recent article "What Is a Particle?" by Natalie Wolchover, published in *Quanta* magazine, discusses the "deeply strange" elementary particles, like photons, electrons, quarks and others, that are considered to constitute "the basic stuff of the universe," and which are considered dimensionless point-like objects, yet have measurable characteristics like charge and mass. The Massachusetts Institute of Technology (MIT) theoretical physicist Xiao-Gang Wen once said, "We say they are fundamental, but that's just a way to say to students, 'Don't ask! I don't know the answer. It's fundamental, don't ask any more.'"

In this case, serious replies to the question "What's the point?" include "a collapsed wave function," "a quantum excitation of a field," "an irreducible representation of a group," "vibrating strings" and "what we measure in detectors." Clearly it is difficult to use language to describe what is essentially an abstract mathematical entity, descriptions of which nevertheless seem to exhibit some kind of understanding about a natural event in space-time.

For astronomers, who analyze radiation from many parts of the electromagnetic spectrum from very remote objects, the issue of time confounds discussion of location and distance, for a galaxy (or for that matter nearby objects in space, like our moon and other planets in the solar system) is observed in its past, recent or remote, there being no universal *now* or point of time. The *when* of an event depends on its *where* as we observe it.

In a lighter vein, we live in a world of wonders, as did the three brothers who inherited their father's cattle ranch and renamed it Focus. When asked why they had chosen this odd name for their ranch, they would always explain that it was the point where the sons raise meat.

Sorry.

November 20, 2020; revised August 25, 2021

30

Mathematical Discoveries

Some curious new information about prime numbers (those whole numbers only divisible by themselves or 1) has recently been reported by mathematicians interested in number theory.

It is well known that all primes greater than the first few (like 2, 3 and 5) must be odd numbers and end in one of only four possible digits: 1, 3, 7 or 9. Primes often occur in pairs separated by a non-prime (like 17 and 19, or 29 and 31), and it has been conjectured, but not proven, that there are an infinite number of these prime pairs, each pair separated by one other number.

We might expect that it would be equally probable that for a prime ending in any of the four possible digits, the prime following it would be equally likely to end in any of the same four possible digits. But as it happens, this seems not to be the case. Curiously, it has now been shown that the following prime is *less* likely to end in the same number as the previous prime than in one of the other three. How come? Nobody knows.

To describe this situation as a recent mathematical "discovery" raises questions on the abstract nature of numbers and suggests that such a finding is based on something latent in the *idea* of a number. As humans we have the capacity to recognize physical instances of numeration, like the five fingers of our hands or the eight arms of an octopus, but prime numbers seem to represent a higher order of abstraction, based not on physical observation but on divisibility, and to consider probabilities such as the likelihood of successive primes ending in particular digits suggests a still higher level of abstraction.

Science Nobelist Roger Penrose poetically invoked the deity in describing abstract mathematical concepts as "God's own design," which recalls the concept of persistence of objects as "ideas in the mind of God" by the eighteenth-century Irish bishop, philosopher and scientist George Berkeley, known for his idealist philosophy, who maintained that reality consists only of minds and their ideas.

Mathematical "discoveries" may not be ideas in the mind of a god, but being abstract, they are clearly different from other concrete scientific discoveries, like finding unknown planets from Newton's laws of motion or the recent finding of the Higgs boson, predicted by the standard model of theoretical physics.

January 28, 2020

31

Academic Philosophy and the History of Ideas

Isaiah Berlin (1909–1997) was born in Riga, Latvia, and became a naturalized British citizen before the Second World War. Considered a major thinker, he is variously thought of as a philosopher, historian of ideas, political theorist, educator, public intellectual, moralist and essayist. He famously left the philosophy faculty at Oxford, unhappy with their analytic approach to academic philosophy, to devote himself to what interested him more than linguistic analysis and epistemology: the history of ideas. In this sense, Berlin came to be thought of as "the non-philosopher's philosopher," authoring a stream of essays addressing a wide range of issues, including politics, history, esthetics and others.

Berlin's 1958 essay "Two Concepts of Liberty" is considered the fundamental interpretation of the meaning and value of political freedom, and his formulation of "value pluralism" led to the development of the idea of tolerance as an ethical justification for celebrating human diversity. Forever a stranger in a strange land, as a Jew from Eastern Europe he was acutely sensitive to being an outsider wherever he went, both before and after the mid-twentieth-century Holocaust. His famous essay "The Hedgehog and the Fox" (1953), inspired by a fragment of ancient Greek poetry, simplistically divided polymaths (foxes) from specialists (hedgehogs) and has since become a popular meme.

Berlin was a brilliant conversationalist and lecturer and defended reason and liberalism as a mode of thinking. Though opposing political extremism in all forms, he controversially sided with the US in its opposition to communism and was in turn duly criticized for supporting American military interventions, confounding a struggle for independence in Southeast Asia with the threat of imposing a rigid economic system. His Zionist sentiments, too, now appear less acceptable, but as he was a Jewish survivor from Eastern Europe, one can understand and perhaps forgive.

Although analytic philosophy has faded in importance at Oxford, as well as at many American universities, and *metaphysics* has seemingly become less of a dirty word, Berlin continues to be celebrated as a major scholar on campus, where one can attend the annual Isaiah Berlin Lectures, receive the Isaiah Berlin Visiting Professorship or relax on the Berlin Quadrangle of Wolfson College. Fine details of epistemological issues, such as the "essence of meaning," may now seem remote and lacking in interest for the non-specialist in academic philosophy, but their contributions to the philosophy of science cannot be denied.

As an undergraduate student in the mid-twentieth century, I was enrolled in what was known as "humanities," a mixture of areas like philosophy, history, literature, sociology, political studies, belief systems, etc., all subsumed under the commonly understood label of, in Berlin's words, the "history of ideas." Like Berlin, but before I had ever heard of him, I started off in an academic philosophy department that focused on the school of logical positivism, involving the close examination of language, eschewing any connection to such areas as existentialism, religious studies, idealism, ethics or traditional metaphysics.

Also like Berlin, I gradually realized that academic philosophy was not my cup of tea because it was dismissive of these other areas that interested me at the time, although professor Herbert Feigl, one of the founders of the Vienna Circle, seemed to soften the rigid views of the logical positivists. Calling himself a "logical empiricist," Feigl rejected those thinkers that insisted there must be "something more," such as an *élan vital*, or life force, as coined by French philosopher Henri Bergson, including all forms of theism. Nor did Feigl accept the reductionist views of "nothing but" touted by those who felt all forms of thinking were merely linguistic conventions invented by humans to account for the existence of ideas. He famously quipped that logical empiricism rejected both those who asserted either "something more" or "nothing but" and instead celebrated empirical science as descriptive of "what is what" and truth based on the criterion of intersubjective testability or verification.

That was good enough for me as a brash twenty-year-old in 1954, and after working for a number of years in observational astronomy, I decided to pursue a career in *doing* science, not just talking about it. Since then I have studied and worked in science, though I continue to think of myself as one whose primary intellectual interests have been, like those of Berlin, the history of ideas and, as with Feigl, a regard for natural science and experimental verification as key approaches to resolving the Gauguin identity questions of who, from whence, and to where we are going.

October 11, 2021; combined with the essay
"Philosophy and Science," October 16, 2021

32

The Late Super Mario

This essay is not about *Super Mario*, a platform game series created by Nintendo, featuring their mascot, Mario, a form of digital entertainment designed to divert children's attention away from relating to the natural world. The late, *real* super Mario, Mario Bunge (1919–2020), was a physicist, philosopher, defender of science and citizen of the world. His 2016 memoir *Between Two Worlds* is a 408-page, densely written and somewhat obsessively over-detailed personal account of his long and productive life and academic work, beginning in Argentina and ultimately continuing in Canada, where he was known for his unique and at times controversial contributions to the philosophy of science at McGill University in Montreal.

Receiving his early training in science in Argentina, Bunge's first academic appointment was as a professor of physics at the University of Buenos Aires, where he taught quantum mechanics. But his interest in philosophy eventually led him to the broader study of logic and the meaning of scientific enquiry. Eventually leaving Argentina for political reasons in 1966, Bunge found a congenial social and intellectual environment in Canada, where he remained until his retirement, continuing to write prolifically about the nature of scientific knowledge, while participating in various congresses, colloquiums and seminars throughout the world.

Throughout his career, Bunge was distinguished with some twenty honorary doctorates and achieved worldwide respect for his humane ideas, rejecting pseudoscientific and unverifiable systems of belief, rigid religious and political ideologies and also psychoanalysis, which he viewed as unscientific and fraudulent.

I met Bunge in 1956 at his home near Buenos Aires, where we talked about our mutual interests in science, philosophy and music. He was thirty-six at the time and already a full professor of physics, while I was only twenty-two, just beginning my research as astronomer in Argentina, a political exile from the US. Our paths never crossed again, but when I learned of his death last year at the age of 100, I bought his memoir, learned more about his academic and family life over many years, and reflected on how both our lives had become more fulfilling after settling in Canada.

I regret never having met Bunge again, who, unlike me, became a distinguished philosopher and scholar, yet his life story resonates with my own thinking and ideas about science, religion and politics. He was my own Super Mario — not a game, but a living fellow humanist.

March 2, 2021

33

Derrida, Bunge, Feigl

Cultish metaphysics, emanating from the turgid and abstruse writings of the French *Pied-Noir* philosopher Jackie (a.k.a. Jacques) Derrida, attained popularity in the late twentieth century, particularly among literary critics, with assertive sloganeers repeating ill-defined and nonsensical philosophical word salads derived from Martin Heidegger, Edmund Husserl and their ilk. Peter Salmon's new biography of Derrida, *An Event, Perhaps*, details Derrida's life from his birth and childhood in colonial Algeria to his relocation in metropolitan France, and traces his intellectual path out of structuralism's prevailing rejection of human-centred philosophy into what became known as deconstruction.

Occluded in a fog of impenetrable obfuscation, deconstruction can be thought of, according to Salmon, as "an approach to understanding the relationship between text and meaning." Purportedly useful in understanding diverse subjects such as literature, politics, religion, music, and education, even this definition of deconstruction still doesn't convey a clear sense of what it is or does. Instead, it may be easier to define, like Derrida himself, what deconstruction is not: a method, a critique, an analysis or post-structuralist.

As we attempt unsuccessfully to understand clearly what all the fuss is about, the problem with defining deconstruction appears to be one of language, not the ignorance of the questioner. Analytic philosophy regards the deconstructionist enterprise as fraudulent and misleading, metaphysical gobbledygook, in which language is used to sound impressive but lacks a clarity of definition.

That being said, Derrida must be commended in one area: for modestly not allowing his photograph to be taken standing before a wall of books to serve as a pictorial representation of an intellectual wizard, pimping deconstruction. In comparison, philosopher of science Mario Bunge's comprehensive and rather self-serving memoir *Between Two Worlds* displays on its front cover the good professor posing in a cardigan, looking relaxed before the groaning shelves of his personal library, and on the back, another photograph of him seated before his typewriter, looking serious and composed behind horn-rimmed glasses, ready to argue the finer points of exactification theory, the background of the photo, of course, being more shelved tomes. Having read both the biography of Derrida and the memoir of Bunge, I much prefer to follow the example set forth by Jackie, not Mario.

Within *The Murder of Professor Schlick* by David Edmonds, the photographs of the philosophers of the Vienna Circle all appear to be studio portraits, with the exception of my old professor and friend Herbert Feigl, who is seated, relaxed on a rock somewhere in the Alps, dressed for hiking, with a twinkle in his eyes. I could provide my hapless biographer (if any) with my picture, seated on a motorcycle in riding attire, with a similar twinkle in my eye.

March 8, 2021

BELIEF

34

Witchcraft and Montague Summers

English author Augustus Montague Summers (1880–1948) was known for his scholarly studies on the occult and for notoriously claiming to believe in the existence of demons, vampires and werewolves. A serious scholar, in 1928 Montague produced the first English translation of the fifteenth-century manual the *Malleus Maleficarum,* which provided instructions for religious inquisitors for interrogating the many unfortunate, often elderly, women accused of witchcraft.

In his study of the late Middle Ages, Dutch cultural historian Johan Huizinga described the fifteenth century as the apogee of the persecution of witches, the concepts of magic and heresy having become conflated at this time. Notably, these persecutions occurred most often in remote mountainous regions like Switzerland and Scotland, the latter perhaps being the origin of scenes with witches in Shakespeare's *Macbeth.* The very accusation of witchcraft was often itself considered evidence of the accused's demonic possession, and denial led to cruel tortures forcing confession, followed by exorcism, so absolution could then be kindly offered before execution. Thus their "souls" could be admitted to "heaven."

A bizarre example of an eccentric queer Englishman, much like his predecessor and author of *Hadrian VII,* Frederick Rolfe, Summers considered himself clergy, and dressed as a Catholic priest, though he was never ordained as such. Only possessing the minor title of deacon in the Church of England, he briefly worked in Bristol before being accused of pederasty.

Summers's primary religious interest, however, was in occult subjects, and this eccentricity is displayed in his books *The History of Witchcraft and Demonology* (1926), *The Vampire: His Kith and Kin* (1928) and *The Werewolf* (1933), all written in a bizarre and unusual style, openly displaying the author's belief in the reality of these subjects. Summers's biographer, Father Brocard Sewell, observed:

> During the year 1927, the striking and sombre figure of the Reverend Montague Summers in black soutane and cloak, with buckled shoes, could often have been seen entering or leaving the reading room of the British Museum, carrying a large black portfolio bearing on its side a white label, showing in blood-red capitals, the legend 'VAMPIRES'.

Nevertheless, Summers's translation of the *Malleus Maleficarum* from the original Latin was considered accurate by experts. He was elected a fellow of the Royal Society of Literature in 1916 and was known for producing important studies of the Gothic fiction genre. Unlike Rolfe, Summers's eccentricity was not associated with a severe personality disorder, though in the prudish words of Rolfe's biographer A.J.A. Symons, both Summers and Rolfe were "unlucky men in whom the impulses of passion were misdirected."

June 21, 2021

35

Prayer

Expiation is defined as "the act of making amends or reparation for guilt or wrongdoing" — atonement. In the case of a minor, or venial, sin, a Roman Catholic priest may offer absolution and instruct the sinner to formulaic repetition of prayer, commonly Hail Mary or Our Father.

While hope is an attitude of positive expectation, prayer is a verbal expression of spoken or written language addressed to a deity. But prayer is more than just ritualistic behaviour and may include magical words or phrases intended to facilitate a desired outcome. For example, when a Roman Catholic priest consecrates the wafer during Holy Mass, he speaks the Latin phrase *Hoc est enim corpus meum* (literally, "This is my body"), while simultaneously performing gestures specific to the magical procedure, like making the sign of the cross. The characterization of the phrase as seemingly gibberish by those unfamiliar with Latin is the origin of the term *hocus-pocus*.

Of course, incantation is not limited to Roman Catholicism, and formulaic repetition, usually accompanied by other ritualistic behaviour, is practised in many different settings. For example, secret societies (or "societies with secrets," like Freemasonry) may employ specific words or phrases to convey a shared secret meaning, facilitating group bonding. Words and phrases shared among limited groups of individuals often become popular beyond their initial use. Over time, slogans may emerge from such repeated vocalizations, such as Adolf Hitler's *Deutschland erwache!* (Germany, awake!) in the twentieth century, or Donald Trump's Make America Great Again in the twenty-first, both promoting nativism within specific national entities.

Common to all these expressions is emotional baggage of some kind, be it personal desiderata or group expectation, and a wish for the future to be different from the current state of affairs, whether that be an episode of individual unhappiness or shared dissatisfaction with current circumstances among a group. Over the ages, these manifestations of magical thinking have contributed to unhappy consequences like wars, genocide and general human misery.

Not all chanting is necessarily addressed to a singular deity, however, nor is it always negativistic in terms of outcome. Non-monotheistic religions may also express hope, as with ancient

Greek sailors appealing to Poseidon, specifically, as the god of the seas, to protect them while on the water, rather than to the Hebrews' Yahweh, who was believed to rule over all natural phenomena.

July 22, 2020

36

Delusional Disciplines

Otherwise known as the Abrahamic faiths, Judaism, Christianity and Islam all arose in the southwestern corner of Eurasia as organized religions founded on earlier monotheistic beliefs, such as Zoroastrianism, practised well before what became known as the common era, formerly designated BC, for "before Christ," supposedly — and inaccurately — dated from the birth of an itinerant preacher born in a barn in Bethlehem in an eastern province of the decadent but still powerful Roman Empire.

Following the cruel execution by crucifixion of Jesus of Nazareth for his adhesion to the "Abrahamic vision," his followers split into a number of competing cults, dividing the then prevailing population of monotheistic believers known as Israelites. The most successful of these cults was one promoted by one of the Israelites' former persecutors, a Pharisee known as Saul, who apparently experienced an epiphany after falling off his horse (or perhaps suffered what sounds like an epileptic seizure) during a trip to Damascus; performed a *volte-face*, promptly changing his name to Paul; and undertook a series of trips to promote his vision of Jesus as having been the actual son of their deity. As a divine intervention, this was supposedly forecast in Hebrew scriptures, promising eternal "salvation" to those who accepted Paul's visions.

This cult became known as Christianity, the second of the three Abrahamic faiths and eventually the official religion of the late Roman Empire and beyond, demanding adhesion to its tripartite god by all on pain of everlasting damnation and the fiendish tortures of hell. (The third of the Abrahamic faiths, Islam, came later, but that's another story.)

Christian theology is the systemic study of their god and its divine attributes, usually taught at universities and seminaries as an academic subject. Acerbic controversies abound among initiates and occasionally make their way into non-academic circles. Even the respectable *Times Literary Supplement* (*TLS*) featured a review of Notre Dame University theologian David Bentley Hart's latest book, *That All Shall Be Saved*, wherein Hart propounds the unusual Christian view that none will suffer the eternal tortures of hell, regardless of religious belief, and offers several closely reasoned arguments to support his bizarre non-traditional interpretation, seemingly denying purgatory as a repository for contrite sinners.

Hart's book was carefully reviewed and politely critiqued in the *TLS* by Anglican priest and theologian Vernon White, visiting professor in the Department of Theology and Religious Studies at King's College, London. White's carefully couched review takes no overwhelming stance against Hart's conclusions but openly criticizes the style of Hart's writing, whose opinions are presented "passionately, polemically, rhetorically, and repetitively. He is completely certain about it. In his own words, Hart asserts, 'I suffer no doubts regarding my views.'"

Hart has surfaced before in the pages of the *TLS*. In an article about philosopher Isaiah Berlin, Hart derided Berlin as "fraudulent" in his discussion of Johann Georg Hamann, an early proponent of anti-enlightenment reasoning, provoking outraged letters to the editor and a subsequent retraction of the adjective with a new offering of "superficial." Hart's problem seems to reflect his vantage point as a specialist scholar and theologian, in comparison to Berlin's more relaxed attitude as a historian of ideas — an example of a narrowly focused hedgehog disdaining a broadly oriented fox.

The tendency of Hart to publicly overvalue his own opinions and devalue those of others suggests to me (as a psychiatrist) concerns about certain unwelcome features of Hart's personality, but not having directly assessed his mental status, I must refrain from any further comments about the man. But the controversy illustrates the academic divide between the fields of religious studies, whose target of study may be the more general area of religious belief among humans, and theology, a sectarian discipline presupposing the existence of a deity and a manifestation of the delusional beliefs common to all three Abrahamic faiths.

I must personally declare, echoing Hart's hubristic confession, "I suffer no doubt regarding my views."

October 27, 2021

37

The *Tanakh*: The *Hebrew Bible*

The *Tanakh* is a canonical collection of twenty-four Hebrew scriptures, written by different authors, organized into three sections: the Torah (translated literally as "Instruction" or "Law"), Nevi'im (Prophets) and Ketuvim (Writings). Its presentation is similar, but not identical in organization, to what Christians call the Old Testament, considered to be divinely inspired words forecasting the account in the *New Testament* of Jesus being the offspring of their deity. Many phrases from the English translation of the *Tanakh* will be readily recognized by anyone familiar with the history of ideas and popular culture, like "reaping the whirlwind" from the book of the minor prophet Hosea, or from Genesis 3:19, "You are dust and to dust you shall return."

The last work of the late Italian scholar and polymath Roberto Calasso (1941–2021), *The Book of All Books,* was recently reviewed in the *Times Literary Supplement* by Italophile Tim Parks, who characterizes Calasso's rendering of the *Tanakh* as "a kind of adult version of a children's Bible," a rewriting of Jewish scripture and the familiar stories of Sunday schools in Christian churches, like Jonah and the whale, Daniel in the lion's den and the rest. There is nothing new in Calasso's text, however, and Parks notes that a reader may as well just read the Bible itself, "something that few people nowadays actually attempt." (I feel somewhat entitled to comment having recently done exactly that.)

Aptly titled, *The Book of All Books* recognizes the structure of the *Tanakh*, which purports to be a true history of the Israeli people, as a collection of separate books written by different authors over a long period during the last millennium before the common era. Some of the historical material can be dated by linguists, but the earliest events, like the origin of matter, life and humans themselves, are mythological. Some books, like Proverbs and Psalms, are ignored within Calasso's book, and he rearranges the familiar order of others, beginning with historical accounts of judges and kings rather than the usual story of the Creation, in Genesis, and its aftermath. Familiar stories about the first of mankind, the Garden of Eden, the Tower of Babel, Noah and the flood, etc., are deferred to the end.

A concluding chapter forecasting the arrival of a capital-M "Messiah" seemingly injects a taint of Christianity into the otherwise traditional Jewish scripture. This seems an unwarranted contamination, though in his review, Parks charitably suggests it is consistent with Calasso's previous writings about mythologies.

It was a unique literary experience to read the entire *Tanakh* now in these "end times," but having no desire to repeat the experience, my next long read may be something less serious, perhaps the entertaining P.G. Wodehouse's Jeeves romps, or maybe James Joyce's challenging novel *Finnegans Wake*.

March 20, 2022

38

Messiahs

The concept of a messiah as a saviour or liberator historically arose, and was first described, in the Jewish bible, referring to a king or high priest traditionally anointed with perfumed oil considered to be holy. Within Hebrew scripture, however, there was no reference to a single individual called "the Messiah." At the time of Babylonian exile, this term came to be associated with a future imagined king, anointed with the oil to rule over their deity's kingdom, but not God himself, unlike the concept of the "son of God" found in the theological tradition of Christianity, which co-opted the Jewish biblical tradition and assigned to the itinerant preacher known as Jesus of Nazareth the role of the Messiah.

The respected *HarperCollins Bible Dictionary* contains a lengthy discussion of the development of Christianity from first-century Jewish cults, by Joseph A. Fitzmyer, professor emeritus of biblical studies at the Catholic University of America. In his entry he wrote that in Romans 9:5, from the *New Testament*, St. Paul identified Jesus as "the one who has fulfilled the Palestinian Jewish expectations of old" and that "the Christian confession that Jesus is 'Messiah' played its primary role in Christian debates with Judaism."

In the world of music, performances of George Frideric Handel's 1742 oratorio *The Messiah* have come to be regarded as an annual Christmas tradition, like coloured lights, ubiquitous recordings of soppingly sweet carols, liquid "Christmas cheer" refreshments, and festive home and office gatherings of tipsy celebrants adorned in Santa suits and elf hats. The text of Handel's *Messiah* was written by English landowner and patron of the arts Charles Jennens (1700–1773) and was assembled from bits of the King James Bible and the Anglican Book of Common Prayer. It was literally Christian propaganda, allegedly proving that the life of Jesus was prophesized in the Old Testament, or Jewish bible.

In a less spiritual and more sinister sense, the concept of "messiah" has come to be applied to populist politicians like Mao, Hitler, Duterte and Trump, each promising to create a happy future for their believers, and to enact cruel punishment for their real or imagined enemies.

Hallelujah, everybody!

December 18, 2021

39

God's Dog

Following his previous role as watchdog of adherence to Catholic doctrine in the renamed papal inquisition, Pope Benedict XVI was dubbed "God's Rottweiler" by the *Daily Telegraph* in the UK at the time of his accession to the papacy. A sympathetic recent biography by Peter Seewald presents Benedict XVI as the reluctant choice of the Vatican clique of reactionaries following the second Vatican Council, which had relaxed some of the long-standing rigid church rules. Seewald describes him as a "docile character whom one wishes hadn't been called to a bureaucratic life to which he wasn't suited." According to Seewald, he was not a fierce Rottweiler but rather a bookish prelate who only wanted to read and pray, and his decision to retire must have been a great relief, allowing him space from all the Vatican shenanigans among his colleagues.

Though a great exaggeration of Benedict XVI's influence to effect changes in society, Diego Marani's counterfactual dystopic thriller *God's Dog* alludes to Benedict XVI's reputation as an ultra-conservative. Set in a near-contemporary Italy, the novel features policeman Domingo Salazar, an inspector and agent of the Vatican, now the political authority presiding over the "Catholic Republic of Italy." Marani imagines that in the "New Concordat," the catechism of Benedict XVI makes offences against chastity a crime, along with homosexuality, masturbation and fornication, affirming "the citizen is conscience-bound to ignore the orders of the civil authorities which run counter to the demands of the moral order, to fundamental rights or the teachings of the Gospel."

Civil unrest follows. Eventually the political uproar stabilizes, and most anti-papists emigrate rather than engage in opposition. A few remain, however, fomenting unrest, becoming the targets of Vatican police enforcers like Inspector Salazar. Motivated by the outlawing of euthanasia, for example, a dissident organization, involving spies and secret agents, inserts itself into care homes and hospitals. The leader of the organization's father, confined to a palliative care unit in which pain and suffering are treated with prayer instead of medication, is used as bait by the police to entice the leader's return from exile and capture.

But the basic plot in *God's Dog* arises from the investigation of another dissident organization, deemed terrorists by the Vatican police, who plan to disrupt the public canonization of Pope Benedict XVI in St. Peter's Square in Vatican City amid papal dignitaries, undercover agents, Swiss Guards and a crowd of believers. Throughout the course of his attempt to foil their plot, Inspector Salazar is identified as an enemy policeman by the terrorist group and closely escapes kidnapping and potential assassination.

Beyond the anticipated thrills of a plot with regular spices of money, drugs, violence, criminality and even sex (!), there is more than just the entertainment of a good yarn in *God's Dog*. Inspector Salazar keeps a diary, recording his thoughts about moral issues like abortion and euthanasia. He writes,

> We persist in trying to bring the Church to the people. We ought to be doing the reverse: making it more remote, not more accessible. Restoring a sense of mystery... Man must feel *impelled* to revere God, to placate his wrath. Fear is of the essence.... We should begin by reintroducing sacrifice....

Although Salazar grapples with tough issues through the pages of the work, allegedly the account of a literate and loyal policeman in a fictional theocratic state, the perils of imposing such an ideology also resonate in today's world, where freedom of dissent is already imperilled in more than one jurisdiction.

September 15, 2020; revised September 3, 2021

40

Angels and Saints, Part I: "Angels"

Eliot Weinberger's recent book *Angels and Saints*, like the Christian deity itself, is tripartite. The first part of this recondite but accessible work consists of an extended and exhaustive essay about those once popular but imaginary entities known as angels, referred to and debated by theologians since the initial formation in the declining Roman Empire of the Jewish cult that came to be known as Christianity.

In the first part of Weinberger's book, he begins with a review of who and what the angels may be, noting that little has been written about them in scripture. In fact, they appear in the scripture less than two hundred times. No indication is given of the supposed origin of angels, and there are contradictory descriptions of their appearance by believers reporting visions. Angelic deserters, or fallen angels, were once thought to be numerous, and demonology became associated with theology in the Middle Ages, presumably to account for the presence of evil.

The second section of Part 1 of Weinberger's book addresses the concept of personalized, or guardian, angels. In a 2008 survey (of Americans) by Baylor University's Institute for Studies of Religion, more than half of all adults, including 1 in 5 of those who say they are not religious, believe that they have been protected by a guardian angel during their life. Clearly the idea is popular, though these results perhaps say more about the level of education in the US than about theology.

Specific orders of angels are reviewed in the third section, including *seraphim*, "anonymous workers in the hive of heaven"; *cherubim,* of which there are only two, both "holdovers from Mesopotamia"; and *thrones*, which, while not specifically mentioned, are thought to be found in passages from scripture, from which general concepts of their powers and virtues are inferred. Archangels represent a special category of messenger angel who delivers important messages from God, like announcing her parthenogenesis to the virgin Mary, though Weinberger slyly wonders what a "routine message" from the deity might be.

The fourth section concentrates on a specific book, *The Celestial Hierarchy*, which reveals hierarchical stages, or levels, among angels. It was written at the time of the church fathers by the author Dionysius the Areopagite, who, coexistent with Paul, was briefly mentioned in Paul's Acts (c. 170 CE). (Later, Dionysius was called St. Denis in Paris.) *The Celestial Hierarchy* appeared in many translations and was copied throughout the Middle Ages by monkish scribes, and later mentioned by the thirteenth-century Dominican philosopher Thomas Aquinas, who admitted that our knowledge of the angels was imperfect. Even the later Martin Luther opined that Dionysius was devoid of any scholarly merit.

The fifth section of Weinberger's chapter on angels presents a kaleidoscope of named guardian angels, along with the specific targets of their angelic attention, such as Rempel, the "angel of clouds," and Asmoday, who "teaches mathematics and can make men invisible." Then there was John the Baptist, who was "not a man but an angel." This panoply of nearly a hundred different angels and their liaisons is an impressive collection of instances of a supernatural religious belief in non-human entities.

The sixth section consists solely of two verses written in an unidentified language alongside their English translations. The verses, which refer to a distant paradise with "bright angels," are described as having been found in 1898 in "a small unpainted wood church in a clearing on the Fraser River." The location suggests the likely language of the text is that of a Canadian First Nation in southwestern British Columbia. In the first verse, the angels appear to be standing, while in the second they have trod on the riverbank.

The seventh and final section on angels is a brief paragraph revealing the lurid anatomical details associated with the appearance of a recent supine human corpse in which the settling of blood and other bodily fluids, as caused by gravity, resulted in a patterned mottling of the skin on the upper back, appearing suggestive of places of attachment of wings and reflecting the belief of the Cathars, a Christian dualist, or Gnostic, movement that thrived in southern Europe between the twelfth and fourteenth centuries, whose members believed that humans were fallen angels.

Why go to the trouble of discussing angels anyway? Like unicorns, they are imaginary, but we don't think of ourselves as possessing a personal unicorn, or of monocerosal interventions in human affairs. Angels, however, are ideas of beings that have been assigned intercessory powers by those who literally believe in their existence. This makes them fair game for one like Weinberger, who is interested in the history of ideas, and relevant to considerations of the limitations of human knowledge.

April 12, 2021

41

Angels and Saints, Part II: "Saints"

Unlike angels, saints were real people, not imaginary beings. They were individuals possessing unusual powers, authenticated by ecclesiastic officials. Sainthood thus is a real attribute, implying holiness or some exalted state certified by a religious authority. *Saintly* as an adjective therefore implies behaviour approved by the tripartite Christian deity commonly called God by adherents of that religion.

In the second part of Eliot Weinberger's book *Angels and Saints*, the reader is presented with 130 short biographical sketches of saints, each entry headed by their name and location and the dates of their alleged powers, and followed by an account, ranging from a single sentence to several pages, indicating the reason for their inclusion in Weinberger's volume. While most sketches are relatively brief, some extend into deep biographical histories. (Many of the saints are also identified in the periodically updated Penguin collection first edited by Roman Catholic hagiologist Donald Attwater in 1965.)

The biographical details of the saints, when available, are at times fantastic, even bizarre, as with Genesius of Arles (France,

d. 303 or 308), identified only as "a decapitated martyr, his body was buried in France but his head was transported 'in the hands of angels' to Spain, where he is invoked as a protection against dandruff." Other biographical descriptions are equally piquant, like Robert Bickerdyke (England, d. 1586): "an apprentice laborer, he was seen in a pub buying a priest a glass of ale and was executed in York." This is stated as a matter of fact, and no speculation is proffered about whether martyrdom was an appropriate sequel for this offence.

In fact, there are no explanations for any of the reported activities meriting sainthood among most of the sketches. Rather, there is an overwhelming preponderance of curious and at times outlandish circumstances, whose inclusion by Weinberger was seemingly for that reason alone and not for the presumed holiness of the sanctified. He apparently assumes an intelligent reader is able to recognize the absurdity of elevation to sainthood.

Early saints were often those martyred for their steadfast beliefs, historically depicted by excruciating techniques that curdle the blood of the reader, whereas saints of the Middle Ages are more often subjects of fantastic marvels described in oral accounts. Many of the more recent specimens seem to have been more rigorously vetted for the attested "authenticity" of miracles performed.

In one celebrated instance, alleged holy works of the early twentieth-century St. Thérèse in France became an industry, producing paraphernalia of devotional items of all kinds, such as "devotional cards to carry in a purse or wallet, postcards, lithographs, calendars, souvenir albums, exercise books, writing paper and blotters, short silent films, lockets, charms, badges, brooches, scarf pins, necklaces, bracelets, medallions, napkin rings, and gift boxes to hold them." All these items were produced by a single company whose sole offering is products associated with St. Thérèse.

St. Thérèse was canonized in 1925 by Pope Pius XI, apparently because of her immensely popular book *The Story of a Soul*, which inspired millions of believers. According to Attwater, "Miracles and answers to prayer were attributed on all sides to her intercession in Heaven." At her canonization, half a million people gathered to celebrate the occasion in St. Peter's Square. The cult of St. Thérèse, which facilitated a populist right-wing Catholic conservatism, had connections to the Vichy collaborationist government during the Second World War, with the nuns even producing images of Thérèse showering rose petals on pro-fascist leader Marshal Pétain.

Weinberger closes his enumeration of selected saints with a three-page account of the current process to proclaim sainthood on Edvige Carboni (Italy, d. 1952), who reported that an angel placed a crown of thorns on her head, producing stigmata. Carboni had visions and was allegedly tormented by the devil, while the Virgin Mary told her she was to "suffer for the conversion of communists." Not having assessed her formally in a mental status examination, I cannot assign a psychiatric diagnosis, but some form of thought disorder was likely present, resembling that seen in clinical schizophrenia.

The psychosis seems to have persisted, and Carboni wrote that after Holy Communion on a spring day in 1951, Jesus told her, "This morning the soul of Benito Mussolini has entered into Heaven." After she died, a Vatican committee found no objection to proceed to sainthood, so she was proclaimed Venerable in 2017 by Pope Francis. The following year he approved attribution of a miracle to her intercession, the final step before beatification. Presumably the process continues.

April 17, 2021

42

Holiness and Decay

Holiness and saintliness are attributes often associated with physical features different from those of ordinary humans, at times with hints of immortality following their demise, such as the delayed onset of olfactory evidence of death.

In the dismal chill predawn in this year of the waning plague, I awoke early with morbid thoughts of Titurel, the former leader of the Knights of the Grail in Richard Wagner's majestic final opera *Parsifal* (1882). In Act I, Titurel's aged voice is briefly heard from offstage, commanding his sinful son Amfortas to uncover the Grail, a symbol of holiness. Years later, in Act III, Titurel has just died, and the Knights carry his corpse in a solemn funeral procession. During the procession, the wise and virtuous old monk Gurnemanz relates to the astonished Parsifal how, despite his holiness, the aged Titurel had died: "*Er starb, ein Mensch, wie alles.*" (He died, a man, like all).

Then there was Zosima, the holy and benevolent Russian monk venerated by the novice Alyosha Karamazov in Fyodor Dostoevsky's profound final novel *The Brothers Karamazov*. Zosima dies, and his corpse, awaiting burial, begins to emit the foul "odour of corruption," announcing the onset of decay and reminding the other monks that, however holy in demeanour he had been, he too was a man, like all. Whether expected or not, decay cannot be avoided, however holy the deceased may have been in life. For those who doubt, the odour of decay will disabuse them. Holiness does not guarantee incorruptibility.

Fictional holiness, of course, is not a feature of the natural world, but a label at times applied to those individuals of a spiritual disposition who show compassion and kindness towards others. Both Parsifal in Wagner's opera and Alyosha in Dostoevsky's novel exhibited these qualities and behaviours and were esteemed by others. Non-fictional holiness is different. Notoriously, the suicide bombers of two decades ago, disparaged as terrorists by most of us who reject their values and despise their actions, were perceived as holy by their confederates.

Immanuel Kant and Isaiah Berlin would have characterized this tragedy as an unavoidable consequence of the "crooked timber of humanity," assigning to inborn human nature a failure of empathy, which leads to conflict and misery. Notably, the late Jan Morris considered the ultimate human virtue to be the expression of kindness. An enlightened sentiment worthy of emulation by all, perhaps accompanied by an understanding of holiness as being but an ideal, and its actualization for some as a goal, not an end state. Though, like others, we will all decay, cremation will at least eliminate the odour of corruption.

December 31, 2020; revised September 11, 2021

43

Chastity

According to legend, Catherine of Alexandria (c. 287–c. 305), who became a Christian around the age of fourteen, supposedly converted hundreds of people to Christianity before she was allegedly martyred at about the age of eighteen at the hands of the Roman emperor Maxentius. Yet according to scholar Donald Attwater, as written in his 1965 compendium of saints, "There is no trace of her name in records of early martyrs, nor any other positive evidence that she ever existed outside the mind of some [unidentified] Greek writer." More than 1,100 years after Catherine's alleged martyrdom, Joan of Arc identified her as one of the saints who appeared to and counselled her, and a cult was formed around her.

Catherine's name appears in a recent review by Clair Wills in the *New York Review of Books* of *The Chastity Plot* by English PhD candidate Lisabeth During, in which she is described as "the patron saint of unmarried girls," a pagan who had a dream in which the Virgin Mary asked her if she would like to be married to Jesus. Since she didn't like any of the other suitors offered her at the time, she agreed, but first she had to convert to Christianity, and thus ended up being martyred.

St. Catherine's holiness was praised, and as brides of Christ are destined to keep themselves for the afterlife, so are chaste women to save themselves for marriage. This became the common Christian expectation, if not always the practice. She gained a large female following as a focus of devotion and model for proper feminine behaviour during the late Middle Ages and after.

During blames Calvinist theologians for introducing the idea of chastity as a Christian ideal, though redefining it as chaste love between married partners, echoing the grudging acceptance by St. Paul of sexual desire as a necessary evil arising from human sexuality.

Wills, a fellow at the Columbia Institute for Ideas and Imagination in Paris, identifies the main thrust of During's book as identifying chastity as a "means of maintaining sovereignty over the self through refusal."

Both During's book and Wills's review, however, are exclusively concerned with chastity as an issue in heterosexual relations; same-sex couples never appear, and there is only a passing mention of a single instance of male chastity with Hippolytus in Seneca's play *Phaedra*. And of course, there is no mention of the likes of the pre-Christian King David, with his multiple wives and concubines.

December 29, 2021

44

Original Sin

In classical Athens in the fifth century BCE, the historian Thucydides wrote his *History of the Peloponnesian War* devoid of any divine explanation. It is the earliest surviving atheist narrative of human history.

In the Hellenistic age of the third century BCE in Greece, and extending into the early Roman Empire, atheism was widespread, owing to the popularity of Epicureanism, a belief system that considered gods at best remote and uninterested in human affairs. But after the Christianization of the Roman Empire, beginning with the conversion of Emperor Constantine in 312, Christianity was proclaimed the official religion of the empire and all were ordered to follow it. This put an end to philosophical atheism for over a millennium, and remaining polytheists were considered atheists and exterminated. Atheism could serve no purpose now that the "true Christian message" had been revealed and enforced.

Stability in the late Roman Empire was achieved by the state religion of Christianity through the introduction of a form of thought control, and by focusing attention on the afterlife instead of the ambient vicissitudes of day-to-day living. In these present times of social unrest, theocracy again seems to many an attractive means to preserve stability. A future descent into barbarism awaits the gentle souls who believe we all should just become more tolerant of those who differ. The rude beasts now slouching towards democratic societies are religious fanatics of different colours, and mutual destruction lies ahead for all; regrettably, hatred is the common denominator of our species.

Calls for a new Spanish Inquisition type of world order proliferate, seen as much in the rise of Hinduism in Modi's India as among the uneducated believers in the American southern states and elsewhere, such as in rural areas of Canada, calling for a Christian theocracy. Meanwhile, fanatic Islamists in Afghanistan enforce control of half the population by the other half, dividing humans by gender as well as belief. Zionist extremism in Israel is another echo of this process of religious and social control. Not limited to the Abrahamic faiths, the ongoing persecutions and killings of the Muslim Rohingya people in Myanmar is being perpetrated by the non-Muslim Burmese military. These back-and-forth conflicts clearly have perpetuated the poison of religious belief throughout recorded history.

As an alternative to religious belief, state atheism becomes more attractive as states turn to religious absolutism. In China, promotion of atheism looks capable of resisting the growth of religious fanaticism at this time, but it too will eventually collapse as the wheel of Ixion revolves, fuelled by greed and driven by human nature, otherwise known as original sin to those of the Abrahamic monotheist religions. This concept presupposes an initial Eden-like existence of humanity, from which we are now all exiled, owing to consuming the metaphorical apple from the "Tree of Knowledge" that our "Creator" warned us against.

Perhaps the creators of artificial intelligence in today's world should be aware of the inherent problems of humanity associated with their goals.

August 16, 2021

45

Buddhism and Mindfulness

In an essay in *Aeon*, Buddhist scholar Alexander Wynne summarized what is known about the sage known as the Buddha ("the Awakened"), who emerged from a small town on the border between India and Nepal in the fifth century BCE. His early years are obscured by myth, but historical sources suggest he founded an austere cult based on meditation and withdrawal from the vicissitudes of ordinary life. The Buddha taught a "dialectic of silence" and avoided engaging in speculation about issues like the meaning of life, the relationship of man to nature, or issues of morality. He cherished the virtues of a state of equanimity, mental or emotional stability or composure, calmness and equilibrium.

This is not unlike the advice given by the Canadian physician Sir William Osler (1849–1919), who sensibly cautioned, "The best way to develop a good sense of equanimity is not to expect too much from the people among whom you dwell." Fair enough. Just be kind if you can, and don't fret if you're not appreciated.

Buddhism has influenced Western culture since at least the nineteenth century, not only in novels like those of Herman Hesse but more recently in the late twentieth century, in works such as the 1979 opera *Satyagraha*, composed by Philip Glass, which references non-violence as a mode of confronting external threats. Wynne suggests the Buddhist approach of regarding the world as dependent on the activity of our minds and sense facilities could be considered "a useful aid to modern cognitive science."

In psychology, mindfulness meditation, derived from fairly recent Burmese innovations, is a therapeutic approach to subjective distress caused by life's problems. The meditation path, which has gained ground since the early 1900s, is a form of Buddhist meditation that is seen as leading to awakening and can involve intense meditative retreats. Although it was initially presented as an alternative to psychotropic medication, recent work in psychedelic facilitation of equanimity has led to the increased use of agents like psilocybin and lysergic acid.

Teachings of the sage of ancient India remain relevant in the troubled world of today, given the multiple social and individual challenges associated with stressors like global warming and viral pandemics. Enforced individual isolation may be assuaged by engaging in these techniques derived from Buddhist thought.

December 30, 2020; revised August 29, 2021

46

Entheogens: Intoxication Legitimized

An unsolicited announcement recently arrived in my mailbox, inviting me to participate in a "conversation" about redefining psychedelic intoxication as a religious experience: "Harvard Divinity School's Center for the Study of World Religions will be hosting a conversation about Psychedelic Chaplaincy, sponsored by Esalen, Riverstyx Foundation, and Chacruna."

As with cannabis, as attitudes continue to shift, enormous profits are also likely to be made in non-medical so-called wellness markets. "Wellness" is a trillion-dollar global industry. As stated by Scott Nelson of the Forbes Business Development Council, "Whether that's home microdosing kits, spiritual retreats, or 'therapies' for people feeling lost and without direction, where there's a disposable income, there's a psychedelics company with an answer."

Sound familiar? It should, and before long there will surely appear offers like the above to train users in using and administering substances that induce a change in consciousness, either "serious," as in divinity schools promoting entheogens (pharmaceutical agents that produce simulated religious experiences), or simply recreational, allowing the user to enjoy "trips" that offer a view of the world different from the usual grime and crime of daily living in a society hell-bent on its own destruction.

One of the difficulties with therapeutic use of psychedelics is the difficulty in predicting the outcome. While some patients using them perceive great benefit and believe they produce a positive, even religious, experience or epiphany, this varies by the individual. As the University of British Columbia author and activist Sheldon Goldfarb commented in his review of my memoir *Foxtrot*, "Some people take LSD and turn into fools; others become psychiatrists."

Living as we do in a capitalist monetary system, with profit to be made by facilitating service to an eager population, we can anticipate that "business schools," offering diplomas and perhaps "advanced degrees," will soon cash in on the desire to make a profit from punters searching for a quick fix for ennui, the promise of swallowing a psilocybin pill or a tab of LSD being cheaper and more convenient than costly hours on the couch of a psychoanalyst, perhaps gaining insight but with no guarantee of attaining a realistic world view consistent with what we can see around us.

No need to worry about the collapse of civilization or the destruction of the environment if you can "change your consciousness" when desired. Cloaking the products in an aura of religious facilitation reassures the user that the practice of selling guaranteed states of feeling "one with God" is both appropriate and desirable, and above all, profitable. But facilitating an epiphany may backfire. St. Paul thought that he beheld a deity, but he later identified the love of money as the root of all evil. (How about that, Mr. Forbes?)

The Harvard Divinity School should consider aligning itself with the Harvard Business School, for ending legal prohibition of psychedelics (as suggested in California — where else?) will result in the same phenomenon of enthusiastic merchandising as did the end of the prohibition of alcohol in the previous century. I foresee yesterday's "opium dens" masquerading as tomorrow's "churches," offering sacraments of magic mushrooms and their ilk to their parishioners.

Another recently received letter, this one from Michael Pollan, invited me to subscribe to a newsletter called *The Microdose*, breathlessly announcing,

> There has never been a more exciting — or bewildering — time in the world of psychedelics. What just a few years ago was an obscure corner of clinical and neuroscientific research has blossomed into a vibrant scientific field, yielding promising new treatments and important insights about the mind and brain. That research has already spawned an entirely new industry, with hundreds of startups, all with different ideas of how best to commercialize psychedelics.

Economic determinism wins over mystical insightfulness — entheogens can make you rich!

As a retired psychiatrist, I am reminded of one of my professors of psychiatry in 1976, who told the class that he had tried LSD and indeed had experienced profound insights, but realized after the experience that these insights were all trivial.

February 18, 2021; revised October 29, 2021

47

Angels and Saints, Part III: "The Afterlife"

The third and final part of Eliot Weinberger's *Angels and Saints* concludes with the following parable:

The Afterlife

> In the Glögnitz Valley of Carinthia they used to tell, until quite recently, the story of two sheep herders, old friends, who made a pact: When one

died, he would come back to tell the other what he saw. Not long after, one of them indeed died and did indeed come back.

He said: "It's not what I thought it would be. It's not what you think it will be. They're very strict about the rules."

Then he disappeared.

Since no further explanation is given, the reader is invited to reflect and to supply one — some formulation of the lesson or the moral suggested by the parable. A reader engaged in this exercise will necessarily draw images from their own memory and world view once they have considered why the returnee may have found the afterlife strange and unexpected, and specifically what was meant by its "rules."

The Austrian shepherds probably would have thought of the parable in terms of the Christian afterlife, comprised of the saved, happily ensconced in paradise, and the damned, miserable in their inferno. But a contemporary reader may more likely imagine a possible non-heavenly, terrestrial utopic society wherein all one's needs were met, or its opposite, a dystopic and unhappy earthbound future for failed humanity. Or perhaps both simultaneously, as seen in works of dystopic fiction like E.M. Forster's creepy short story "The Machine Stops" (1909) and in tales of other writers that envisage a future human society controlled by presumably beneficent machines endowed with artificial intelligence.

The concept of a utopian future is not limited to fictional representations. A political system based on Marxist utopian communism (like *Juche* in the Democratic People's Republic of Korea?) has strict rules against criticism, leading to the "disappearance" of dissidents. In such a supposedly perfectly stable society, failure to obey can provoke punishment or banishment, i.e., disappearance. And there is always the Spanish Inquisition, which knew how to deal with those dissidents, or the Stasi in the old German

Democratic Republic, the Soviet NKVD and the current "socialism with Chinese characteristics" of Xi and his Chinese Communist Party cohort.

The moral or lesson of Weinberger's parable might be something like "Be careful what you wish for — you might get it."

April 18, 2021

SELF AND SOCIETY

48

Narcissism, Writing and the Human Condition

Once we are gone, we are all sooner or later forgotten — out of sight, out of mind — and for most of us this is an unwelcome realization. Some may seek to perpetuate the survival of their names and accomplishments, a form of self-gratification.

While narcissism may not be included in the list of deadly sins, the desire to see one's ideas and associations in print could nevertheless be considered prideful, much like the gratification received from medals and ribbons adorning the chests of military "heroes" and the inevitably obese and self-satisfied dictators who have succeeded in clawing their way to the summit of power.

As I find myself writing essays, and subsequently circulating them among others, it seems timely and reasonable to consider the motivations for engaging in this type of activity and form of communication. In other words, why bother?

To speculate overmuch on the future of humanity seems unwholesome, and to promote this among others is unkind, for unwelcome knowledge is often conceived of not as a tasty intellectual idea, but rather as a horror best evaded or ignored. Jeremiah knew that, and the preacher voiced it to the multitudes anyway, unswayed by nay-sayers. And what are the ethical consequences of publishing opinions that nobody wants to hear? I find it is much like finding yourself lost and yelling for help in the middle of a forest, but the trees aren't listening. Instead, they are relentlessly being "harvested," i.e., chopped down.

Some authors may be reluctant not only to publish unwanted opinions but also to share them by way of promotion and marketing, the process necessitating the hiring of agents to convince punters to exchange their cash for the privilege of reading about their own impending demise. This sounds ridiculous, but there it is. Narcissism thus may have a hidden relationship to economic determinism, for profit is the overall goal of every industry, including publishing, from the publicist engaged to promote sales to the bookseller (who is often not a book reader) and the authors themselves, compelled by tax authorities to reveal the pittances obtained from this process after all others have taken their cut.

A Roman emperor (Nero? Vespasian?) was said to have replied to a citizen who complained to him of having to pay for the use of the public toilets, "The money doesn't smell."

So, there you have it. The love of money, said to be the root of all evil by St. Paul, made explicit. The cause of it, individual narcissism, itself a characteristic of the human condition. A built-in universal drive to compete for success, an idea attributable to none other than our old friend Arthur Schopenhauer and his concept of the world as will and representation.

Familiar examples of this self-promotion in the natural world are often found in features such as mating displays that utilize colour, as in birds; posture and odour, as in mammals; and even sound, as in birds and some insects. The species of *Homo sapiens* is no exception, leading to commercial exploitation in industries of beauty, physical fitness, fashion and cosmetic surgery, all designed to attract a mate for the purpose of sexual reproduction, understandable in the context of Darwinian evolution and the descent of the species.

Self-promotion may be motivated by the desire not only to find a mate, but also to enhance wealth and/or power over others. This is commonly seen in advertising, with the promotion of a product inflated to suggest if not universality then at least terrestrial eminence. For example, a nearby diner seeking vegetarian customers announces its nut burger as "world famous."

Similarly, a small airport in a Canadian town not far from the US border describes itself as an "international airport," despite having no scheduled service from outside the country. Nevertheless, it welcomes small personally piloted aircraft from south of the border to land and take off. This type of promotion prompted Houston, Texas, to rename its international terminal (to avoid comparison) the Houston *Intercontinental* Airport.

At its most blatant, self-promotion is commonly seen wherever the phrase "world class" appears, prevailing on potential punters with an aura of exclusivity and fame enjoyed by the particular brand of watch, vehicle or organization being extolled. In the literary world, this usage may appear in a blurb or short promotional phrase appearing on the jacket of a book, enticing a possible buyer to fork over the cash, rewarding both the author with a royalty and the publisher for the work of editing and printing.

January 14, 2022; combined with the essay
"Self-Promotion and 'Blurb-ery,'" June 12, 2021

49

Philanthropy

The office of the United Nations High Commissioner for Refugees (UNHCR) does commendable work internationally, providing aid to those displaced by the horrors of war in the Middle East and elsewhere. Being inadequately funded by the non-united nations of the world — including Canada, the US and the UK, all profitably selling their weapons of war — the UNHCR solicited public donations with an ad displaying the picture of a pitiful Syrian child, huddled in a blanket, helpless and destitute, apparently having just wept and with no tears left to shed. A powerful and no doubt effective image, it was ubiquitous on internet websites such as the BBC, and one's immediate impulse was to whip out a credit card and give what one could as a philanthropic gesture, the modern equivalent of tossing a coin at a beggar.

Paul Vallely examines the psychology of philanthropy and giving in his new book *Philanthropy: From Aristotle to Zuckerberg,* thoughtfully reviewed by Martin Vander Weyer in the September 2020 *Literary Review.* Vallely distinguishes between two kinds of giving: reciprocal, or "giving by the heart," emotionally driven by contact between the giver and the recipient; and "effective altruism," large-scale philanthropy that uses market forces to effect aid to regions or entities. The former is like Pope Francis and the latter, Bill Gates.

Many projects of effective altruism have been successful, such as the Gates Foundation's support for HIV prevention in India, as well as their 2016 pledge to invest $5 billion over five years in support of health and anti-poverty initiatives in Africa. Possible motives of the billionaire giver, who sponsors well-meant programs of nutrition, medical care and environmental protection to impoverished areas, may well arise from feelings of guilt, a way of assuaging discomfort with their disproportional wealth and vast holdings as they watch the majority struggle for daily existence.

Not mentioned in Vander Weyer's review are the allegedly "philanthropic" donations to universities, which endow the establishment and uphold their operation as "MBA mills." Coyly described as "business schools," promising wealthy careers in sales, marketing and the like to its graduates, these universities inevitably bear the names of their benefactors, advertised and eulogized in right-wing publications like the *Economist.* For example, the Schulich School of Business at York University in Toronto is endowed by Canadian businessman Seymour Schulich. The wealthy Sackler family of pharmaceutical notoriety donated to cultural institutions like museums, galleries and universities, but their names were erased once it was revealed that their profits were derived from encouraging the sale of addictive opioid drugs.

A wickedly amusing anecdote of philanthropy is the case of a natty British businessman who finds a dishevelled beggar on the ground in a London tube station, with a sign scrawled beside his cap that reads *Falklands Veteran*. Outraged by the obvious neglect of perhaps a fellow ex-warrior, the businessman says he will complain to his MP and gives the fellow a fiver. The grateful recipient replies, "¡Muchas gracias, señor!"

August 17, 2021

50

Blaming

We commonly assign blame for wrongdoing as a response to unwanted events, like natural disasters (a diety), wars (an instigator), planetary destruction (human greed), human extinction (overpopulation), aging (time), or breaking a bone by accidentally dropping a motorcycle on one's foot (oneself, i.e., carelessness). The purpose being to deny personal responsibility for the event(s) and to assign it elsewhere, to another person, to an organization, or perhaps even to a deity, with the unwanted event labelled an "act of God." Is it then but a matter of assigning blame according to the severity of an unwanted event that leads us to direct blame at someone or something for causing the problem?

It starts early. In childhood, normal egocentric disobedience is discouraged by parents, teachers and other authorities, hopefully to promote appropriate behaviour among peers and adults. Thus, ordinary naughtiness by the young, like being unkind to others, may become the target of blame by others with some disability, like deafness or poor balance. For adults, civil and criminal law recognizes degrees of culpability for unwanted behaviour, assigning blame for crimes to their perpetrators, whose offences may range from parking infractions, misdemeanours and felonies to premeditated murder. Associated punishments in turn extend from simple fines for minor misdeeds to imprisonment for major crimes, and sometimes, for the greatest, even execution.

Apart from the usual childhood misdemeanours and adult

disagreements and illegal behaviours are religious infractions or sins, which may be minor, as in the careless omitting of a portion of some ritual behaviour, or major, like cursing the deity. Some ordinary sexual variations have been defined as sins by religious authorities and confounded with normal human behaviour, often leading to legal oppression and punishment, invoking the concept of blame to protect and promote some imagined idea of social stability, as in the current dictatorship of Vladimir Putin in Russia, with its institutionalized homophobia.

This apparent universality of blaming historically suggests that the behaviour may be an inbred reaction of humans to unforeseen negative events, explicitly described in, but not limited to, ancient literature, the Jewish bible and later Christian doctrines. Natural disasters like plagues (mentioned by Camus in his novel *The Plague*) and earthquakes (such as the one in Lisbon in 1755, referenced in Voltaire's *Candide*) were attributed to punishments of sinful mankind by a deity.

Non-supernatural explanations for these disasters and other unwanted events in the world first appeared with the rise of natural philosophy (science) after the Enlightenment in Europe and with the rise of Marxism, which blamed social class structure and capitalist economics for the oppression of the poor by the rich.

Perhaps so, but while it makes sense to blame human beings for causing the catastrophe of global warming, plagues can only realistically be blamed on infectious disease agents, and the blame for earthquakes is clearly attributed not to a supposed deity but to continental drift and (ahem) faults in the crust of the Earth.

March 6, 2022

51

A Northern Tragedy

The *Whitehorse Star* newspaper recently reported on the death of K——, who was tried for second-degree murder and convicted of strangling his wife in the town of Whitehorse a quarter of a century ago. At that time, being the only psychiatrist in the Yukon Territory, I was asked by the prosecution to examine his mental status, later testifying as an expert witness at his jury trial.

At the Whitehorse Correctional Centre, I interviewed K—— in depth about his life history, sexuality and marital adjustment and searched for any symptoms of mood or thought disorder. I concluded that he was neither clinically depressed nor psychotic, though he was remorseful about his actions, and fully intact in terms of his ability to undergo trial for his crime. He could only state that his action had not been premeditated, but was rather a spontaneous loss of control when his spouse had mocked his masculinity.

At the trial, after affirming to tell the truth, I explained my findings to the judge and jury, and suggested that whatever the decision by the jury, K—— would have to live for the remainder of his life with the knowledge of his deed, for as an affirmed Christian believer, he had failed to obey the commandment of not killing. Having killed the one he once loved surely must have created substantial, lifelong, lasting remorse.

K—— was fortunate in his defence, having secured the services of a competent specialist in forensic psychiatry from British Columbia, who made an excellent presentation of how extreme stress can cause an otherwise normal person to "suddenly snap" and engage in extreme behaviour. The jury was convinced, and the judge awarded a sentence of five years for manslaughter, commenting, "I doubt the punishment will satisfy those family members."

It didn't.

Family and friends of the victim were outraged at the time and continue to blame the justice system for not having condemned K—— to a more severe punishment.

In recently printed comments about the case, besides grieving the loss of a friend and family member, most continued to blame the justice system for not providing sufficient retribution, many expressing personal satisfaction with K——'s demise, and one even voicing the hope that for his misdeed he would suffer eternally in hell.

K——'s crime was not premeditated, like that of Raskolnikov in Dostoevsky's great novel *Crime and Punishment*, but spontaneous. I personally believe the verdict and punishment were just, and while the wish for vengeance is understandable, the basic flaw lies in the human condition, what Immanuel Kant called "the crooked timber of humanity." Given sufficient stress, we are all capable of such actions, all of us are potential murderers. This killer needed punishment for his crime, yes, but also compassion, not vengeance.

July 23, 2021

52

Compensation

The American Psychological Association defines *compensation* as "the substitution or development of strength or capability in one area to offset real or imagined deficiency in another." It may be also considered *overcompensation* when the substituted behaviour exceeds what might actually be necessary in terms of level of compensation for the deficiency. For example, learning about a phenomenon and writing an essay about it can be a form of psychological compensation for one's admitted initial ignorance. Writing an entire book, then, might be an overcompensation.

Compensation may be a conscious or unconscious process. In his classic psychoanalytic theory, Sigmund Freud described compensation as a defence mechanism that protects the individual against the conscious realization of such deficiencies. We all notice this behaviour in others when it's blatant, as when young men "show off" with noisy cars and motorcycles, but it is often less evident to oneself, such as when one, having degrees in science, opts to study psychiatry as an attempt to correct oneself of one's own failure to understand the unwelcome or bizarre behaviour of others.

Compensation may also refer to the legal concept of (usually monetary) restitution for a real or perceived loss, damage or suffering as the result of, for example, a lawsuit alleging medical malpractice subsequent to a patient's death or loss of function. The technical issues arising in tort actions of this nature may involve conflicting medical judgments between physicians, accusations of venality and the creation of ill will among colleagues.

The issue of compensation for injury becomes even more convoluted when consideration is given in responding to the demands for justice by those of racial, religious or other minority status, for real or perceived historical injustices. Governments may formally apologize and remove statues and plaques commemorating those understood to have engaged in practices now considered cruel and worthy of financial or other forms of compensation for behaviour once thought acceptable but now become reprehensible. Conflicts over these issues may lead to unrest and tend to damage social cohesion.

July 28, 2021

53

Resilience

There are always many stresses associated with life, especially in these days of coping with a worldwide pandemic, with realistic concern given to one's own risk of infection, sickness and death. On top of the physical health risks associated with contracting the virus, compulsory isolation breeds loneliness. For many without a partner, this loneliness can be exacerbated, and even for those with partners, social distancing may aggravate pre-existing conflict.

When professional help is sought for someone in distress caught in this situation, cognitive behavioural therapy (CBT), a psychological approach to reduce individual distress associated with mild to moderate states of anxiety and/or dysphoria, may be used. CBT promotes resilience, which is our ability to recover from the inevitable stresses of life. Practising resilience is not about avoiding disagreeable events, but about learning techniques that allow one to cope with such events as they occur. One such program of the Canadian Mental Health Association, Bounce Back, is a free virtual mental health skill-building program that helps people over the age of fifteen who are experiencing significant psychological distress affecting their social or occupational functioning. The program is widely available across Canada, usually upon a medical referral and necessary screening to exclude those with major depression or a psychotic illness requiring medication and a different form of treatment.

For some disadvantaged groups, being told to be resilient is tantamount to denying their perception of being selectively mistreated and telling them to stop complaining. Some sensitive members of devalued minority groups appear to be easily "traumatized" by perceived slurs, and complain bitterly about treatment by the majority, whether the slur was intended or not. In this way, the idea of resilience is often linked by the majority to the repression and persecution of a devalued minority group. According to the *Times Literary Supplement*, a complaint by a reader about the editor of a respectable poetry magazine, for allowing the printing of the "n-word" in an accepted contribution, led to the editor's firing. While understandable, this type of punishment seems excessively severe and interferes with harmonious living among those whose opinions differ about race, religion, sexual orientation, gender, national origin or some other minority status.

Name-calling, though disagreeable and at times threatening, is universal, and though reprehensible, is not only unkind but probably ineradicable. Insults exchanged between players on opposing teams in physical sports like ice hockey, for example, have traditionally been used as a psychological weapon, and the recipient of such verbiage is expected to shrug it off, i.e., be resilient, and to not complain to the referee about their hurt feelings. And children running to their parents wailing that a peer has called them a "bad name" may be told to "get over it," with emotional resilience promoted with the refrain, "Sticks and stones may break my bones, but names can never hurt me." (Physical violence, however, is another matter.)

Outspoken American actor and author Ethan Hawke, when asked how he handled bad reviews, replied, "I can take bad reviews as a writer, because if critics don't like it, then really they just don't like the way my brain works, and I'm OK with that. I meet people in restaurants that hate me. And 70 million people voted for Trump. There's no accounting for taste."

Yet the CBC and other media continually and loudly promote a podcast whose title proclaims, *Don't Call Me Resilient*, denouncing the use of the term among those who perceive themselves to be "traumatized" by some kind of slur.

February 10, 2021

54

Mad, Sad or Bad?

The useful but simplistic rhyming trinity of adjectives "mad, sad or bad?" summarizes the basic reasons for psychiatric referral; at least, that is what we were taught in medical school in the mid-twentieth century.

After another four years of training in psychiatry, we learned to master nosology (the classification of mental disorders) and the systems of the *Diagnostic and Statistical Manual of Mental Disorders*, employed by psychiatrists in North America, and the *International Classification of Diseases* codes of the World Health Organization, used elsewhere, and generally by medical statisticians. But these technical niceties are only refinements of the classical trio of "mad, sad or bad," which continues to suffice for most referring sources (also for poets, including opera librettists).

The mid-twentieth century opera by Igor Stravinsky *The Rake's Progress* (1951) was inspired by a series of images by English artist

William Hogarth (1705–1743) depicting the dissolution of an intemperate man into psychosis through drink and the absence of self-control, leading to his institutionalization in a madhouse. The libretto by W.H. Auden and Chester Kallman features a closing chorus singing lines from the French poet Victor Hugo: "Leave all love and hope behind / Out of sight is out of mind."

Outraged by the callous and exploitative treatment of the insane in England in the nineteenth century, enlightened industrialists like the Tukes of York, a family of Quaker innovators, beneficently founded homes in park-like surroundings as refuges for those with disorganized behaviour, where they would be cared for by kindly staff. Over time, these asylums became institutions crowded with clients, and their attendants were not always so kindly. By the mid-twentieth century, admission to these institutions, run by specialized physicians known as psychiatrists, was often involuntary, and they were perceived as a type of prison for those with behavioural disturbance.

Made infamous by American writer Ken Kesey in his shocking novel *One Flew Over the Cuckoo's Nest* (1962) and professionally supported by Hungarian American psychiatrist Thomas Szasz in his iconoclastic book *The Myth of Mental Illness* (1961), the rapid development of pharmaceutical agents successfully targeted mental disorders like depression, anxiety and mood instability and thought disorders, or psychoses. Now seen as redundant and expensive, asylums closed, and community "mental health centres" were formed as oases providing professional care and access to pharmaceutical treatment. Group homes, known as "halfway houses," were established to provide intermediate transitional care for those discharged from governmental asylums into independent living in the community. This approach was reasonably successful in countries where social services were readily available, as in Finland, the rest of Scandinavia and elsewhere in western Europe.

In the UK and the Anglosphere, however, in the interest of cost effectiveness and low taxation, this ideal has become a disgraceful failure. The disappearance of the "insane asylum" and the difficulty in accessing an alternative has led to the proliferation of homeless mentally ill people, sleeping rough in doorways, pitching unwanted tents in public parks and begging for spare change outside of shops in major cities. (The latter is even less of an alternative now, due to an almost universal usage of credit card payments in stores and restaurants.)

The misguided abolishment of asylums has led to a significantly worse existence for the chronically mentally ill, and the supposed replacement of community "mental health centres" are a despicable failure. Kesey trashed the concept of asylums so thoroughly that *One Flew Over the Cuckoo's Nest* did as much for chronically mentally ill patients as *Mein Kampf* did for European Jewry in the Third Reich. Strong words, but I say them as a clinical psychiatrist who directed an acute-care psychiatric ward in Vancouver, BC, from 1985 to 1990. Thirty-two years later, the situation in Canada and the US is only worse.

So much for the plight of the "mad" and the "sad," but what about the "bad"? State executions, known as "capital punishment," of those deemed to be irremediably criminal are sanctioned in many jurisdictions in the US and elsewhere, such as in Saudi Arabia, China and North Korea. Apart from intermittent state killings, multitudes are incarcerated in the US for drug dealing and other relatively trivial offences, in euphemistically termed "correctional centres," some of which are public while many others are privately operated for profit. Another triumph of Adam Smith's "invisible hand."

Worse still, indigent and homeless people who cannot afford pricey lawyers to get them off on discharge or reduced punishment fill up the US prison system, where documented inmates are disproportionally members of racial minorities. Meanwhile, private mental hospitals are naturally always available somewhere for those who can afford to pay for inpatient treatment, targeting the moneyed classes through advertisements in slick publications like the *New Yorker*.

For the rest of mankind, the words from Berthold Brecht's *The Threepenny Opera* (1930) still poetically echo the situation after nearly a century:

> Denn die einen sind in Dunkeln
> Und die andern sind in Licht
> Und man siehet die im Lichte

Die im Dunkeln sieht man nicht

(For the ones they are in darkness
And the others are in light
And you see the ones in brightness
Those in darkness drop from sight)

December 22, 2021

55

Estrangement

Friedrich Rückert was a nineteenth-century German poet and oriental philologist whose poetry of *Weltschmerz* was set to music by Gustav Mahler in a renowned series of orchestral songs that continue to resonate today among those of us from that faraway land known as the past. Of especial poignancy is the lament describing estrangement from the world, *"Ich bin der Welt abhanden gekommen,"* a sentiment expressed by an individual who continues to live in a cultural milieu that has evolved in directions beyond those once enclosed within their own world view.

This feeling is enhanced by social isolation, especially when surrounded by age-related peers. Remaining in what has become no longer a familiar world, we may perceive ourselves as immigrants or outsiders, not only because of geographic relocation but also as a consequence of advanced age. Cultural displacement is further enhanced by a progressive loss of friends and peers who inevitably drop out, not only from mortality but sometimes from the cognitive loss associated with dementing illness.

While one may feel alienated from others in a crowd, this sense of estrangement is further reinforced by the imposition of social isolation caused by public health requirements during the current viral pandemic. Being solitary, without even a companion animal, forces one to increasingly value correspondence with family members and one's few remaining friends.

To some extent, my small personal library mitigates solitude, for the presence of authors like Michel de Montaigne, Alberto Manguel and Isaiah Berlin on one's shelves are welcome passive companions. But books don't hug, or even elbow-bump. Creative writing, however, generates an opportunity to have a conversation with oneself about an idea or an experience that could be examined or explored. But like any creation, it remains but a personal possession until it is shared.

Alternatives to creative activity include distraction and displacement of attention, as ways of avoiding morbid ideation and risk of self-harm. Awareness of a sense of estrangement may, however, prove beneficial, igniting latent creativity that would otherwise have remained occult, concealed behind the fulfillment of daily needs and social activities. Redefinition of estrangement in this way, as not necessarily a negative emotion, might even be construed as psychologically protective if one's creations are deemed worthy by others.

April 8, 2021

56

Fear of Offending

Writing in *The Conversation*, Jila Ghomeshi, professor of linguistics at the University of Manitoba, considered the sometimes-vexing decisions we are compelled to make when addressing a member of a minority group that is, or perceives itself to be, devalued or disrespected by the majority. The title of her essay, "BIPOC or IBPOC? LGBTQ or LGBTQ2S+? Who Decides Which Terms We Should Use?" suggests concern among those sensitive to the feelings of others.

Unanticipated social and grammatical issues involving speaking and writing may surface. As a living language, English continues to alter itself with the passage of time and as the result of migration and the constant shifting of social attitudes. This issue of preferred nomenclature resembles that of pronoun choice, wherein the unwary may unintentionally offend another person who differs in race, religion, national origin, physical appearance, gender identity or some other divisive category. It should be noted that language itself can be thought of as a complicating factor, for the English employment of gendered pronouns is absent in Finnish and spoken Mandarin (though in Mandarin the written characters differ).

Pronoun choice difficulties are illustrated in Ghomeshi's article by the picture of a name tag whose message, displayed in rainbow-coloured words (thus implying sensitivity to sexual or gender identity), is of the self-description of the bearer, clearly announcing "HELLO, My Pronouns Are _____."

Ghomeshi appropriately notes that within different groups in a society, individuals may belong simultaneously to more than one minority, as with a Black lesbian immigrant who complained of not being treated courteously by straight white male policemen and other authority figures. To resent such behaviour is understandable, but as an outsider in her community, it behoved her to exhibit resilience if she wished to be accepted by others, and it was unrealistic of her to expect instant change in the use of language by all unlike herself. Slurs about race and sexual orientation have appeared to diminish over decades in the general population, though new ones may yet arise. The use of pronouns, however, seems more deeply ingrained in speech and writing, changing but little over centuries.

It seems unlikely that those who inadvertently employ language that offends others will necessarily change their ways abruptly, for historically it has been common to use words that may have been offensive to refer to those outside of one's tribe. For example, it was a well-known practice among ancient Greeks to call non-Greeks "barbarians." Because they couldn't speak proper Greek, they instead voiced what sounded to Greek ears like "ba-ba-ba."

May 26, 2021

57

The Full Stop

What the Brits call a *full stop* the Yanks call a *period* — both are used to indicate the end of a written sentence. (Mandarin Chinese employs a small circle at the end of a string of characters to the same effect.) According to a news item quoted in his scintillating blog *So It Goes*, British author John Fleming informs us that to use a full stop, or period, when texting is considered rude by members of Gen Z, a shorthand term referring to those born between 1996 and 2015. These young people consider the insertion of this symbol in a text message to be "a sign of curt passive aggression," according to linguist Lauren Fonteyn, who asserted, "If you add that additional marker for completion, they will read something into it, and it tends to be a falling intonation or negative tone."

The use of texting as a means of communication is emotionally arid as a technique of information exchange, wherein the lack of nuance available in speech or traditional writing impoverishes its users. Circumventing this deficit can be accomplished through the use of special symbols, such as the "sarcasm switch," or /S, used at the end of a post so the reader knows you are actually being sarcastic. This and other emotional nuances may also be inserted by the use of emojis.

Attribution of the symbols to Gen Z suggests that those born in earlier decades lack the ability to understand the conventions and niceties of contemporary modes of information exchange. In other words, members of preceding age cohorts, such as Boomers (1946–1963), Gen X (1964–1978), Gen Y and Millennials (1979–1995), are "uncool," another example of the conquest of language by a younger generation. Genres of popular music also display generational origins, like bebop, jazz, swing, rock, metal, hip-hop, etc. Serious music genres also reflect this, but change more slowly over centuries, such as medieval plainsong, baroque, classical, romantic, dodecaphonic, etc. Perhaps one reason folk music seems to be appreciated among different generations is because it appears to be timeless, unlike pop or classical music, which can be readily identified as belonging to a particular period of history.

Those of us born in the years before 1945 are termed "the silent generation," suggesting disparagement, repudiation and the consignment of one's opinions to what was formerly called the dustbin of history and now is but the dumpster of memories of all the unhappy events wrought by *Homo sapiens*.

May the inheritors of our parlous times survive to appreciate their brave new world. /S

August 31, 2020

SOCIETY AND SELF

58

Isms as Pathogens

The term *social organism* is a sociological concept, or model, wherein a society or social structure is thought of as a living organism. Just as a biological organism can be invaded by a pathogen, causing dysfunction, disease, or even death, so too can a social organism be invaded by an "ism," leading to instability, riots and even revolution. An ism may be defined as a distinctive political or economic doctrine, theory, system or practice; we live in an age of isms, like nationalism, communism, capitalism, imperialism, Americanism, etc.

The historian of ideas Isaiah Berlin gave a talk to a group of scholars in 1966, later published in 2018 as the short essay "The Lessons of History" in *The Cambridge Companion to Isaiah Berlin*, in which he argues that the concept of *progress,* in the sense of ending the imperfections of society by employing isms, is based on the false belief that removal of an obstacle will somehow ensure a better world: Marxists wanted to replace capitalism, neoliberals wanted to replace communism, both wanted to replace fascism, and so it goes.

Fat chance. Forced ideologies are frequently counterproductive, historically leading to the deaths of millions.

Ideological isms can be seen in the beliefs of individuals shared among members of a group, such as political movements agitating for social change. Nationalist leaders like Mao Zedong, Adolf Hitler, Joseph Stalin and Margaret Thatcher promoted their particular isms by drawing into their orbits not only the uneducated but also intellectuals, who adhered, and gave legitimation, to their particular ism, convinced that in doing so, a better world would therefore ensue. In his book *The Captive Mind* (1953), Polish writer, poet, academic and Nobel laureate Czesław Miłosz explored why so many intellectuals were attracted to Stalinism, for example, and to authoritarianism more generally. Among the explanations given were their attraction to the promise of a better future and their need for a "feeling of belonging." In general, this behaviour led to the identification of what was called "cognitive dissonance," or incongruity between thought and action.

In an essay in the *New York Review* in 2010, historian Tony Judt also discussed and elaborated on this notion, citing antecedents in Eastern European literature, such as Stanisław Ignacy Witkiewicz's obscure novel *Insatiability* (1927), of how chemically induced adaptive compliance and elective identities allowed one to tolerate a contradictory lifestyle, saying one thing and believing another. Judt described Miłosz as having thought of two possible explanations. One is from a story in which Central Europeans, facing the prospect of being overrun by unidentified Asiatic hordes, pop a little pill that relieves them of their fear and anxiety. Buoyed by its effects, they not only accept their new rulers but are positively happy to receive them.

The other explanation is that of *ketman*, borrowed from Arthur de Gobineau's *Religions and Philosophies of Central Asia,* in which a French traveller describes the Persian phenomenon of elective identities. Those who have internalized the way of being called ketman can live with the contradictions of saying one thing and believing another, paying lip service to Islam while concealing secret opposition, adapting freely to each new requirement of their rulers while believing that they have preserved somewhere within themselves the autonomy of a free thinker — or at any rate, a thinker who has freely chosen to subordinate themselves to the ideas and dictates of others.

The first of these scenarios is reminiscent of Aldous Huxley's drug Soma in his 1932 novel *Brave New World*, itself anticipating psychedelics; the second is consistent with the Marxist promise of a better future if capitalism could be eliminated by force.

Casuistry? Perhaps so, but worth considering by those interested in the history of ideas, like Berlin, who, like Miłosz, was an intellectual from Eastern Europe at the time of the Cold War. Both would agree with Judt that the chief characteristic of the servile intellectual is "the fear of thinking for himself."

October 24, 2020; revised August 19, 2021

59

Weeds and Purity

A weed is commonly understood to be an unwanted plant, such as a cabbage in a rose garden or a rosebush in a cabbage patch. As slang, *weed* may also refer to marijuana. The verb *to weed* indicates an action taken to remove, usually by hand, said unwanted plant from one's garden.

When grass is planted to serve as an ornamental lawn or perhaps as an athletic playing field, often a chemical weed killer is employed to remove anything that disrupts the visual aesthetic or playing surface. Roundup, the brand name of a systemic, broad-spectrum glyphosate-based and widely used herbicide, is used most heavily on corn, soy and cotton crops that cleverly have been genetically modified to withstand the chemical, leaving only the unwanted plants at the mercy of the treatment.

In 2012 there were approximately five million acres of California farmland treated with glyphosate herbicides, for produce like almonds, peaches, cantaloupes, onions, cherries, sweet corn and citrus. Roundup's toxicity to humans led to lawsuits, and in June 2020 the manufacturer agreed to settle over a hundred thousand lawsuits, agreeing to pay $8.8 to $9.6 billion to settle those claims, and $1.5 billion for any future claims.

Metaphorically, *to weed out* signifies the procedure of eliminating undesirable members of a population to "purify" the remainder.

The practice of sterilization to prevent pregnancy of female humans perceived as abnormal and laws against miscegenation in the US in the early twentieth century inspired the eugenics program of Germany's Third Reich, wherein physically and mentally disabled citizens were "euthanized" to weed out undesirables. This program was followed by the larger process of eliminating all Jews from Europe, the goal being that of consolidating the supremacy of the so-called Nordic, or "Aryan," race. The "weeding out" of subsets of a human population continues today by restricting immigration, a widely pervasive practice used as a means of enhancing national identity in many countries around the world, arising from xenophobia and nationalism.

More personally, but less dramatically, when a dermatologist reassured me that certain sinister-looking skin patches were benign, he poetically described them as "nothing but weeds in the garden of life."

November 8, 2020; revised August 23, 2021

60

Victims, Vengeance and Justice

Those that suffer because of their race, religion, lifestyle or sexual orientation often cry out for "justice," which is entirely understandable, indeed, commendable. But at times the cries may lead to confounding justice with a demand for retribution, otherwise known as vengeance.

Teasing out the meaning of *justice* can be philosophically complex, involving ethical issues that may not be universally shared. Furthermore, the concept is employed differently by those in power and those that feel oppressed. Generally speaking, justice, derived from the Latin noun *justum*, meaning "what is right," implies fairness, but here again there is no agreement about what is and isn't fair in contested judgments, and the legal professions are securely anchored in their guaranteed incomes by those clamouring for justice and seeking (usually financial) retribution.

Justice is often defined by those in power, and as noted by Lord Acton, "Power tends to corrupt, and absolute power corrupts absolutely. Great men are almost always bad men." To exact punishment for actions inflicted upon victims who perceive themselves to have been unjustly treated has been seen as appropriate, though this appropriateness may be suspect when the conflict is between those who won and those who lost a war, for example. The Nuremberg trials of Nazi politicians following Germany's loss in the Second World War is celebrated as just by those who defeated the Third Reich, but not by those who favoured protecting the "supremacy of the white race."

Racism continues to be a visible instigator of oppression, and its victims cry out daily for "justice," though demands for punishment of, for example, apparent racist behaviour by police and other agents of authority, is in effect a cry for vengeance against those accused of racism, as when arrests and treatment of Black suspects by white policemen in the US exhibit different standards of behaviour based on race. While such actions are a daily occurrence in the US, a similar situation may occur vis-à-vis Indigenous citizens in Canada, manifested in lower life expectancy, reduced educational access and punitive imprisonment.

Minorities in other countries face similar or related issues when there is not a homogeneous population. Tribalism and xenophobia are root causes of conflicts among and between nations and seem to be a near-universal tendency among social groups. Regrettably, this behaviour appears to be common to humanity in general. Though differences in race, nationality or sexual orientation may be the sparks that ignite conflict, we all have this inborn demon within us. It can be suppressed, though not totally eliminated, by learning as a child, through parental guidance and early childhood education, to be tolerant of those unlike ourselves. Unfortunately, tribalism and xenophobia can also be stimulated to emerge by demagogues like Adolf Hitler in the previous century and Donald Trump in the present one.

The importance of education in promoting rationality and compassion in adults is reflected in the similar level of earnings among physicians and teachers in Finland, where in 2021, for the fourth year running, Finland topped the list of 149 countries in the World Happiness Report, an index ranked on the likes of gross domestic product, healthy life expectancy and corruption. It should come as no surprise that Finland is renowned for its excellent public school system, universal health care and egalitarian culture. (Canada was only fourteenth and the US, nineteenth.)

October 2, 2020

61

Cries for Justice

The lyrics to Kurt Weill's 1928 Berlin hit *Die Dreigroschenoper* (*The Threepenny Opera*) were written by dramatist Berthold Brecht. Inspired by the 1728 *Beggar's Opera* by English poet John Gay, *The Threepenny Opera* portrays the plight of the downtrodden dregs of society, the disadvantaged, mired in poverty, turning to crime — a socially deprived underclass. An eloquent and educated Marxist, Brecht's lyrics are an exposé of the inequalities between the rich and the poor in the Weimar Republic. Now, nearly a hundred years later, the opera continues to powerfully resonate in our own time as a cry of despair amid the decadent stench of capitalist neoliberalism.

In the opera's "Ballad of Pirate Jenny," an oppressed kitchen worker dreams of vengeance against the town that oppresses her by killing all others before being whisked away to safety, suggestive of the Marxist daydreams of the Bolsheviks before 1917, essentially the mindset of Lenin, Stalin and their comrades. And we know how all that turned out. But such are the lessons of history that are never learned and always repeated. As George Santayana wrote in his *Life of Reason* (1905), "Those who cannot remember the past are condemned to repeat it."

Cries demanding "justice" resonate these days, as racial and social minorities understandably feel betrayed by real and perceived persecution, not only of themselves, but also of their ancestors, and loudly shout for apologies and restitution. Demands of justice for past activities, however, may cause outrage and incitement to vengeance by those historically oppressed, leading first to the desecration of symbols, such as the burning of churches, throwing statues into the sea, etc. In turn, these actions invite retaliation by those whose ancestors were responsible for the historically documented oppressions. Back and forth it goes as violence escalates, and when apologies and appeasement no longer suffice, intervention by the power of rulers is invoked, and when this is not accepted or obeyed, the result is civil disorder and eventually dictatorship, thereby suppressing all forms of dissent.

So ended the unstable democracy of the Weimar Republic — leading to the exile of the authors of *The Threepenny Opera* — and the establishment of the Third Reich in 1933, initially under the promise of restoring law and order in the streets. We know how all that turned out too.

The wheel of Ixion turns, confirming the relevance today of the theory of Polybius, a Greek historian of the Hellenistic period, of rotating systems of government, or anacyclosis, moving from democracy to mob rule and demands for a powerful leader to take charge to restore order. There will always be a Mussolini, a Hitler, or a Trump willing to put things "right" by "popular demand" and cries for stability.

The fundamental difficulty in establishing any stable and enduring system of government, however, lies not in the imperfect written constitutions of modern democracies, but in a fundamental biological drive in the human animal. As Immanuel Kant wrote, "Out of the crooked timber of humanity, no straight thing was ever made."

July 3, 2021

62

The Crooked Timber of Humanity

A Roman senator at the end of the Republic famously wrote that "a nation can survive its fools, and even the ambitious. But it cannot survive treason from within. An enemy at the gates is less formidable, for he is known and carries his banner openly." In other words, a state can be strong and resist external enemies with military might but be powerless when attacked from within by conspirators nibbling away at the political institutions that sustain it.

Marcus Tullius Cicero hit the nail on the head, for while demagogues seeking political power corrupt those who are prepared to fight for it, the fundamental flaw of democracy — or any other system of government — lies not in the minds of supposed "traitors" or their followers, but in the minds of all humans, old or young, male or female, rich or poor, white or Black, atheist or believer. This fundamental flaw lies in the competitive drive to accumulate more (from the environment) to sustain growth and reproduction, a biological imperative expressed in all three domains (superkingdoms) of living organisms, including the common divisions of plants and animals.

Plants compete with one another to secure access to sunlight, directly by shading or indirectly by absorbing heat from another source. Consuming plants or employing predation accomplishes the same end among animals. A balance may be achieved when the reproduction rate of the prey approximates the success rate of the predators, but human interference may upset the balance, leading to unwanted complications, as we see in isolated regions such as New Zealand and Australia, with the introduction of non-native species of animals lacking predators, like rabbits in the eighteenth century.

In the case of humans, once prey themselves for predators like lions and wolves, we now retain our desire for control over others as a form of predation to secure money and power, forming groups to compete for political power by fighting physically, as in war, or politically, as parties vying for power in an electorate.

In referring to "the baseness that lies deep in the hearts of all men," the eloquent Roman senator foreshadowed a fundamental fault of humanity later described by Immanuel Kant. Senator Cicero came to a bad end for voicing his opinion. He was declared an enemy of the state and consequently executed by Mark Antony after the assassination of Julius Caesar. His severed hands and head were then, as a final revenge, displayed openly in Rome.

October 30, 2020; revised August 20, 2021

63

Dissent vs. Stability

Neoliberal social structures endorse dissent as the *sine qua non* of individual freedom and are therefore reluctant to impose limitations on its expression. Yet it is social stability, upheld by law, that is generally acknowledged by citizens as not only desirable but a necessary condition for peace and security, and when dissent leads to disorder it may entail the placing of limits on individual freedom by those with the authority or power to do so.

Of course, dissent is universal, and people will always disagree with each other about what is right and what is wrong, but how this is expressed publicly differs among jurisdictions. A society's high tolerance for dissent can lead to a decrease in stability, as seen in riots and violence in some democratic states, such as in the US and Western Europe, where dissenting opinions are permitted, such as the toleration of different views about Brexit in the UK. Alternatively, restricting dissent, by controlling the media and limiting authorized public demonstrations to only those considered acceptable to the ruling party, as is the case in the People's Republic of China, may promote social stability.

The usual (extreme) example of how limiting individual freedom can promote social stability is that of not being allowed to shout "Fire!" in a crowded theatre for fear of provoking a stampede for the exit. This can be compared to the People's Republic of China's restriction of organized dissent in the Special Administrative Region of Hong Kong, though it is a false analogy, confounding individual behaviour with political demonstration.

When an authoritarian state imposes unpopular restrictions in the name of promoting social stability, such as the censorship of information or free association, in provoking a wave of popular dissent, the consequence of such actions may narrow to either a loss of state power (i.e., revolution) or the crushing of dissent at all costs, such as the Russian Tsar successfully did in January of 1905 (and unsuccessfully in March of 1917), solidifying the revolution leading to the formation of the USSR. A revolt against the state also occurred in Beijing in June of 1989. The Tiananmen Square protests, or the Tiananmen Square Incident, commonly known as the June Fourth Incident in mainland China, were student-led, and like the 1905 revolt in Russia, were ruthlessly crushed by the army under orders from the Communist Party, led by Chairman Deng.

Neither the Westminster form of representative democracy in the UK nor the literal interpretation of an eighteenth-century constitution in the US have managed to prevent the emergence of demagogues intent on forming governments that limit individual freedom in the name of social stability. As I write this, many formerly democratic states have approached one-man dictatorships: the Philippines, India, Brazil, Venezuela, Hungary, and (almost) the US.

November 4, 2020

64

Patriotism

Patriotism, the love of or unconditional feeling of loyalty to the state or nation in which one was raised from childhood, was famously described by Samuel Johnson as "the last refuge of a scoundrel." Many more quotes on this subject are easily accessed on an internet search, almost all of them negativistic and disparaging. This should come as no surprise, for the celebration of patriotism seems to be almost universally scorned by those who have reflected on the subject, from ancient to contemporary writers. This devaluation of patriotism is especially marked in writers who have had personal experience with warfare. Yet politicians continue to extoll the supposed virtues of patriots, commemorating the deeds of valour of a nation's "heroes."

Like most schoolchildren, I was taught to be patriotic about the country of my birth, but I recognized this as a deception after becoming aware of history and politics while an undergraduate at university in my late teens. Some of my acquaintances have maintained they would feel uncomfortable to be without allegiance to any government, but for me, after having elected statelessness as superior to obeying the commands of old men sending off youth to kill or be killed for power under the guise of patriotism, having no nationality created an extraordinary sense of freedom and relief.

The American spy Nathan Hale, who was hanged by British troops during the Revolutionary War, famously said on the scaffold, "I only regret that I have but one life to lose for my country." This epitome of patriotism is praised in history classes in the US to this day but is never accompanied by the description of those promoting the Revolutionary War, allegedly on behalf of liberty and human rights. Thomas Jefferson and his lot, after all, were slave-owning planters, spouting phony praises of equality to induce and confirm patriotism among the masses.

So it has been throughout history, in all wars, abandoning reason in favour of unthinking patriotism, leading to military conscription and the death of millions. To not be a patriot is seen by many as shameful and disreputable, but really should rather merit praise from anyone understanding the origin and consequences of unthinking obedience to those in power.

March 5, 2020; revised September 1, 2021

65

Why War?

Throughout recorded human history, war and its associated horrors have persisted among humans. *Homo sapiens* appears to be the only species of animal to wage war, defined as "deliberate and organized activity for the specific purpose of imposing control over another group." In his recent book *Why War?*, Christopher Coker, who directs a foreign policy think-tank at the London School of Economics, asks and suggests an answer to this very question, and his conclusion is uncomfortable. "It is war," he writes, "that makes us human. It defines us as a species."

Undeniably, boys seem more innately disposed as a tendency towards obvious physical aggression than girls. Encouraged in children's games and in action as adult males, many of them willingly throw themselves into battle, prizing not only the recognition and esteem of their comrades, but above all, "the thrill of feeling alive." Team sports also promote this psychological need; the myth of "fair play" is but a sop to convention. George Orwell once remarked, in a 1945 article in *Tribune* magazine, that team sports were "like war without the shooting." It's not how you play the game, it's whether you win or lose. Dostoevsky noted, "In every one of us a beast lies hidden, a beast of lawlessness let off the chains."

War heroes, driven by their psychological need to excel, coupled with the drive to protect and win respect from their comrades, are publicly honoured with monuments erected to memorialize their actions, and annual national holidays designated ostensibly to celebrate peace incidentally praise the warriors. Every year on Remembrance Day, young cadets, adult soldiers and older veterans march to martial music in annual parades past adoring crowds of onlookers before formally laying wreaths at the base of celebratory monuments as national anthems are intoned.

Coker details the work of anthropologists Michael Wilson and Richard Wrangham on how among and between groups of chimpanzees, as in a zero-sum game, conflict resolution within one band or group leads to an increase in intergroup conflict with another. Psychologically, bonding among members of one group promotes resentment between it and rival groups, a built-in mechanism to foster warfare between them. Coker suggests this observed primate behaviour may also be present in humans.

Individuals may deplore warfare and deliberately avoid participation by exiling themselves, leaving their group or by immersing themselves in pacifist activities like art and science. Yet even these disciplines often facilitate success in warfare by improving lethality of weaponry and/or glorifying martial success. Religions, too, may preach peace but sanction war, as priests may publicly bless weapons, deities may be invoked to promote victory in battle and chaplains attached to military units may promote bonding among the warriors, hopefully leading to their success on the battlefield. The identical processes are seen among their opponents as well, an example of which can be found in the accounts of chaplaincy on both sides during the First World War.

In his conclusion, Coker observes, "Every war is the same: one gives rise to another, as one power falls and another rises in its place. It is an endless cycle in which we find ourselves trapped." War, it seems, is human. In antiquity, both Greeks and Romans practised genocide as a way of eliminating their enemies, such as the destruction of Carthage by Romans in 146 BCE. Biblical scripture describes the early Israelites eradicating their foes with the support of their deity, but this was not limited to their religion. Religious studies scholars describe this activity as common among all tribes at the time.

Organized destruction and elimination of perceived ideological enemies continues to be employed by states like the Third Reich. Peter Ustinov wrote mockingly about the Nazis, but he was right, for genocide has been a human activity throughout the ages, explicitly described in scripture. The victors of the Second World War denied the humanity of their Nazi opponents, whose crime was not so much that of mass murder and genocide as it was industrialization. As humans, this is undeniably a facet of our nature, but then there are other, less unpleasant, qualities of humanity, like trying to understand our place in the universe, our aesthetic creativities and our sometimes-loving kindness.

October 7, 2021; revised November 29, 2021

66

False Flags

The term *false flag* refers to a military strategy in which one side improvises, falsifies or even executes assaults on themselves in the name of their opponents, thereby provoking apparently justifiable retaliation. Such was the excuse for the German forces to descend upon Poland on September 1, 1939, unleashing the European field battles of the Second World War. The "Gleiwitz incident," a false-flag attack on the German radio station Sender Gleiwitz, close to the Polish frontier, had been staged by Nazi Germany on the previous night of August 31, 1939. Along with other similar incidents, the attack was contrived by Germany as a *casus belli* to justify the invasion of Poland, already scheduled for the next morning.

The personal use of nationalist symbols, like flags, which represent a political entity or social group is also a means to proclaim participation in that particular group and no other. But usage of a flag (or another symbol of group identity) is not limited to warfare. Groups within a society may employ them to assert their identities, like rainbow flags associated with sexual minorities, or confederate flags in the US to signify adherence to white supremacy.

In a peculiar display of false-flaggery, apparently inspired by rioting American fascists wrapping themselves in their "stars and stripes," a perverse use of the maple leaf to reject public-health mandates based on science was employed recently by a noisy minority of ignorant Canadian "protesters," who used Canadian flags to reinforce their demands for "freedom of choice" in the prevention (wearing masks) of airborne transmission of viral infection.

Promotion of hatred towards enemies, or support for friends, by displaying flags and other symbols is currently on display internationally, with people, organizations and states announcing opposition to the Russian invasion of Ukraine by using the colours of the latter's flag on private and public sites like bridges and buildings, or in displaying the symbol of a sunflower, the latter's national flower.

While not fact, accusations of threatened false-flag attacks have power, as with false-flag threats of biological or chemical weaponry, often reported as a euphemistically termed "special military operation," i.e., war. In words attributed to the ancient Greek dramatist Aeschylus, what remains clear after more than two millennia is that "the first casualty of warfare is always truth."

March 13, 2022

67

Conscription

Before the emergence of nation states after the fall of the Roman empire, warfare was conducted in the remains of the empire primarily by volunteers and mercenaries, with military occupation couched in an aura of adventure and duty. It was primarily young men who enlisted; it was not obligatory except for slaves, or in the case of impressment, such as the sailors in the warships of England's Royal Navy, achingly portrayed in the Herman Melville novella (and subsequent opera by Benjamin Britten) *Billy Budd*.

When the need for warriors exceeded the supply of volunteers for armies, and if the lure of adventure was not sufficient in providing willing bodies, conscription was instituted, sometimes coyly sanitized as "national service" or "selective service," implying that citizens, by virtue of the geographic site of their birth alone, possessed an inherent obligation to the rulers' state, providing manpower for their wars.

Conscripts were described as "serving," from the Latin *servus,* meaning "slave." In modern contexts, "national service," first documented in the United Kingdom's National Service (Armed Forces) Act of 1939, usually means military service, whereby conscription is a mandatory national service. *Service* is both a euphemism and misnomer, coined by those in power to sanitize the concept of obedience for the powerless. Sometimes an alternative to military service is permitted to those who claim an exemption for reasons of religious faith, but for atheists that are philosophically opposed, refusal is considered a crime and punished by incarceration.

That was my experience in 1954 when I graduated from university, and given the choice of "service" or jail, I chose neither and opted instead for exile, renouncing my citizenship and becoming stateless until I was naturalized as a citizen of another country. Later, changing my name, I returned as a native-born foreign student to pursue a graduate degree in science, but as I couldn't change my birthdate, the authorities tracked me down, at which point I elected a second exile, thus achieving the odd distinction of being exiled twice from the same country.

During the American war of aggression in Vietnam in the last century, many young men came to Canada to avoid conscription, including my oldest friend, now married, retired and living in the UK. He was eventually given amnesty but chose never to return to the US, where, like in all nation states, they continue to celebrate their dead soldiers as brave heroes while those who avoided the "service" are mocked as cowards and losers.

When the American fascists manage to embroil their country in yet another war, and their present volunteer army can only be augmented by reinstituting conscription, we may expect another flood of refugees to again cross the border into Canada.

October 22, 2020; revised September 2, 2021

68

Friends, "Friends" and the Society of Friends

The social medium Facebook facilitates and encourages subscribers to compile a list of "friends" with whom one can exchange messages. Not all Facebook "friends," however, are personal friends, and not all personal friends are Facebook "friends," either. A Venn diagram of two intersecting circles geometrically exhibits the relationship between one's friends and one's "friends," dividing the individuals into four compartments: those people that are one or the other, both or neither. For example, Jack and Joel are both friends and "friends" of mine, whereas Peggy is a friend but not a "friend," and Tim is a "friend" but not a friend. Clear?

And then there is the Society of Friends, a Protestant religious sect founded by George Fox that first appeared in England in the seventeenth century. Commonly known as Quakers — originally an insult because of the members' belief that one should "tremble at the Word of the Lord" — they eventually accepted the term and are now so known, but formally call themselves members of the Society of Friends.

Many members of the Society of Friends emigrated to North America, settling mainly in New England, where they prospered economically and were active in industries such as textiles and whaling. Quakers believe in an "inner Light," an individual sense of divinity, and have historically supported such liberal causes as anti-slavery and the equality of women and men. Refusing military service because of their biblical interpretation, they were allowed alternative service assignments in the twentieth century on religious grounds.

Not all Quakers are theists, and their liberal social views resemble those who call themselves Unitarians. I was a member of the local Unitarian Society in my teens, though when conscripted into the US service, I was denied exemption because my anti-war beliefs were not part of a formal religious obligation. Choosing exile and statelessness, I moved to Argentina, where I had a job waiting for me at the national astronomical observatory.

Living in Argentina in 1956, a Quaker adherent in nearby Montevideo, Uruguay, with connections to my hometown in the US facilitated my marriage to my fiancée Cathleen. We were formally joined in union in a Quaker ceremony, among his community, with no religious official save for a group of Quaker witnesses. We promised to love and support each other as long as we each lived. We did so for fifty-five years, until she died in 2011.

Cathleen and I were lovers and friends, neither Facebook "friends" nor Quakers, but grateful to the Society of Friends for helping us to begin our family.

December 20, 2021

69

Statelessness

Atossa Araxia Abrahamian is a New York–based journalist, senior editor of the *Nation,* and author of *The Cosmopolites: The Coming of the Global Citizen.* Born in Canada, Abrahamian grew up in Switzerland and holds Swiss, Canadian and Iranian citizenship. In 2020, she contributed a review in the *New York Review of Books* titled "The Right to Belong," in which she reviewed Mira L. Siegelberg's *Statelessness: A Modern History* and Dimitry Kochenov's *Citizenship.*

According to the UN, some ten million people scattered around the globe are stateless and are consequently in a precarious position, without formal identification, subject to discrimination and exploitation, stuck with nowhere to go, nor for many the means to do so. Siegelberg asserts that it is common to become stateless by accident, "by being born in the wrong place at the wrong time to the wrong person." For example, empires in the process of falling apart tend to generate statelessness among their (former) constituents, as was the case for the many Russians who fled their country after the Bolshevik revolution and the world wars of the twentieth century. While the "Nansen passport," issued by the now defunct League of Nations, didn't entitle the holder to services, it was at least a form of ID — better than nothing.

While Siegelberg emphasizes the negative aspect of statelessness, Kochenov takes the opposite view, feeling that the institution of citizenship itself is the issue, not statelessness per se. He characterizes citizenship as "a heritage glorifying servility, racism, sexism, and arbitrary exclusion, a status assigned at birth and seldom earned." Citizenship is of course the basis of compulsory military "service," entitling naive youth to the "honour" of dying to promote the national designs of their rulers, leading some to seek exile and statelessness rather than become cannon fodder for the national programs of the US, Nazi Germany, Russia, China, etc.

For Kochenov, citizenship reflects "an authentic bond between the individual and the state, pushing citizenship's inescapable totalitarianism to extremes: not being able to choose your country is feudal, not democratic." Indeed. I would personally have preferred the title of Abrahamian's challenging review to have been "The Right *Not* to Belong."

July 27, 2021

70

Manifest Destiny

This phrase *manifest destiny*, coined in 1845, specifically asserted that the US was divinely destined to expand its control and to spread its concepts of democracy and capitalism across the entire North American continent. The phrase served to endorse settlement from coast to coast by displacing the Indigenous nations, then occupying the entire area. The "Red Indians" were considered to be uncultured savages who needed to be converted to Christianity for their "souls" to be saved, and incidentally, their ancestral lands to be seized by the white settlers to become cultivated and owned as private property. Though this slogan was rejected by those living north of the US, settlers in what became Canada displayed the same attitudes and behaviours in displacing Indigenous people and claiming their land.

American manifest destiny was felt by those embracing it to be kindlier than the actions of European settlers in Latin America, where the local populations were either eliminated or "replaced" through miscegenation through rape and/or marriage, primarily between Indigenous women and their male invaders. The end result in both hemispheres was the annihilation of the cultures of the original inhabitants, or genocide. Similar actions occurred in the twentieth century in Europe when the Third Reich asserted the need for *Lebensraum*, displacing, killing and enslaving Ukrainians, other Slavs and Central Asians, considered to be "racially inferior," replacing them with "Aryan" Germans. Jews were simply defined as an "inferior race" by virtue of their genes and deliberately sent to be eliminated by industrial genocide in the Holocaust.

These more recent unhappy tales resemble the awarding of territory in the ancient Middle East to the Israelites by their deity, as described in the Hebrew scripture (Torah), lands already occupied by others, such as Palestinians. This continues to be a vexed issue millennia later, and it's not surprising that it persists into the twenty-first century.

The recent invasion of Ukraine by Russia in 2022 thus not only has historic parallels with the US manifest destiny of the nineteenth century and with Nazi Germany and its promotion of "racial purity" in the twentieth but is only the latest of a thread throughout recorded human history. Putin's war may be unique in that it is driven not by the desire to exterminate the Ukrainians but to co-opt them into the Russian Empire, whether they want this or not, but whatever the outcome, this dispute will likely persist as an inflamed boil upon the already doomed surface of our unhappy planet.

Environmental destruction, global heating, disease, starvation, and steadily increasing pressure by 7.9 billion people striving to survive at all costs will render armed conflict, like the present war in Europe, merely a side issue, as humanity knowingly continues to promote its own destruction, driven by the lust for power and enabled by capitalist greed.

Sic transit gloria mundi.

February 26, 2022

SOUNDS AND WORDS

71

For the Love of Music?

A splendid recently published overview of classical music by John Mauceri, titled *For the Love of Music: A Conductor's Guide to the Art of Listening*, explores over its nine chapters the development of classical music and how this style embellishes the lives of those who have learned to appreciate it as listeners and performers. Mauceri's text describes how classical music became popular, initially arising from religious observances in Christian churches before gradually expanding beyond these milieux to provide accompaniment to other activities, both for solemn occasions, like requiem masses, and for celebration and entertainment.

The preservation and repetition of music over time is facilitated by usually written instructions indicating how and when to produce certain sounds, either vocally or by means of an instrument, and in what pitch, intensity, sequence and rhythm the sounds should be produced. The gradual development of "families" of instruments, which make sounds of different tones and overtones, like vibrating strings or reeds, percussion, winds, etc., and of musical notation, also helped facilitate classical music's development through several different stylistic and temporal periods.

I have been a fan of classical music for seventy-five years, since middle-level public school, when I learned to read musical notation and how to play string and keyboard instruments. Mauceri's descriptions ring true, enhancing my already wide range of familiarity.

While the tone of Mauceri's writing is more conversational than technical, he doesn't "talk down" to the reader; his style is lucid. Linking time and art, he writes,

> One of the many things that link architectural design with musical structures is that they both must be experienced through time. You, however, control the time spent in architectural spaces, whereas music controls your time. Music never simply is: it is always becoming. Inevitably it also shares a resemblance to storytelling, even when it is called "Symphony no. 2" or "op. 27."

Historically, the development of classical music was strongly affected by the acoustics of the spaces that were available for performance.

Mauceri further elaborates on different kinds of performances, from solo to more complex, such as chamber music for only a few performers to orchestral works for larger groups. He also describes the combining of classical music with dance (in ballet) and theatre (in opera and cinema). Richard Wagner famously promoted combining music with other art modes in his concept of *Gesamtkunstwerk*, meaning a "total work of art," a creation that simultaneously made use of different art forms.

Deliberately restricting his writing to music deriving from western Europe in the past half millennium, Mauceri explains that this was not to deny interest in the music of other cultures or from other historical moments, but rather a choice to focus on the traditional works and performances that are commonly understood to have derived from this particular musical tradition. For example, appreciation of Chinese opera is primarily limited to Chinese audiences, but works by Western classical composers like Beethoven are widely admired and often performed in Beijing and elsewhere in China.

As a conductor of classical music, Mauceri conveys an understanding beyond that of passive listeners and even specific performers, writing, "If there is a future in which only two humans are left, one will be singing to the other, who will probably be playing a makeshift drum. We shall go out with music, because, uniquely, it is who we are." This recent book merits a place on the shelf of every classical music enthusiast.

February 1, 2021

72

Music and Astronomy

The June 2019 issue of the popular astronomy magazine *Sky & Telescope* featured a short essay and review of a 27-page catalogue by Andrew Fraknoi that compiles works of both classical and popular music inspired by extraterrestrial objects and ideas. In Fraknoi's catalogue, titled *Music Inspired by Astronomy: A Resource Guide Organized by Topic,* the entries range from Paul Hindemith's grand twentieth-century opera *Die Harmonie der Welt* (*The Harmony of the World*), about astronomer Johannes Kepler, to *"The Big Bang Theory* Theme" by the Barenaked Ladies and the bluesy rock song "Crescent Moon" by the Cowboy Junkies. Something for everybody; there's no accounting for taste.

Fraknoi sniffingly explains that he has deliberately omitted one of the most common examples of orchestral music relating to astronomy, *The Planets,* a suite by English composer Gustav Holst, because it refers to *astrological* and not *astronomical* phenomena. And though Fraknoi eschews any reference to the pseudoscience of astrology in his catalogue, he does include many listings with references to mythological and allegorical sources, such as those that reference characters from antiquity such as Orion, Perseus, Andromeda and others.

Many of the listings also draw from scripture, such as in Haydn's oratorio *Die Schöpfung (The Creation),* when after a quiet opening representative of darkness, the full orchestra and chorus burst forth with a fortissimo, delivered on the lyrics *"und es war LICHT"* ("and there was LIGHT"). The sudden appearance of light in the biblical story of creation is also found in Act 3 of the third opera of Wagner's *Ring* tetralogy, *Siegfried*, when the hero awakens the sleeping Brünnhilde from her twenty-year slumber with a kiss. Opening her eyes, Brünnhilde belts out her greeting: "*Heil dir, Sonne!*" ("Hail thou, sun.") This joyous start to the lovers' ill-fated romance serves to reestablish the mood of solemn ecstasy, as it immediately follows the inevitable audience laughter induced by the funniest line found in the four long operas, when Siegfried uncovers the apparently sleeping knight, singing in astonishment, "*Das ist kein Mann!*" ("That is no man!").

More profoundly, in one of the "conversation books" Beethoven used to communicate with others when totally deaf in his later years, he wrote an allusion to the famous quotation of philosopher Immanuel Kant — "the Moral Law in us, and the starry Heaven above us" — words inscribed in both German and Russian on Kant's tombstone in Königsberg (now Kaliningrad, but that's another story). Kant went on to write in his *Critique of Practical Reason*, "I do not merely conjecture them [the stars] and seek them as though obscured in darkness or in the transcendent region beyond my horizon: I see them before me, and I associate them with the consciousness of my own existence."

This is what Beethoven acknowledged in his most sublime creations, in the chorale finale of his last symphony, looking up at the starry sky and contemplating his place in the universe. And this is what we all can experience, not only as professional astronomers but as anyone opening their eyes and raising their head outdoors on a clear night.

August 3, 2021

73

Venerating Verdi

In the wine cellar of what was once the Circulo Verdiano restaurant in Parma, Italy, there was a shrine to composer Giuseppe Verdi, whose bust was spotlighted next to a display of framed original opening-night programs of each of his operas. Nearby, a guestbook lay open for visitors who wished to inscribe kind words or mark their presence here, the solemn ceremony enhanced by a recording of the chorus of Hebrew slaves intoning "*Va, pensiero, sull'ali dorate*" ("Go, thought, on wings of gold") from Verdi's early opera *Nabucco*, which became practically a national anthem at the time of Italian unification in the mid-nineteenth century. Born in a village near Parma on October 10, 1813, Verdi became the pre-eminent Italian operatic composer of his time.

In describing Verdi's life and works, English music critic Francis Toye divided his biography into two sections, the first being a thorough but familiar 200-page account of Verdi's life from birth in an impoverished family to his status as a beloved national hero whose operas were and continue to be performed on stages in Italy and worldwide. The second and longer section of Toye's work consists of detailed discussions of Verdi's musical style, his literary and theatrical judgment and his collaboration (as an octogenarian) with fellow composer Arrigo Boito in the creation of his final two masterpieces, *Otello* and *Falstaff*. Toye analyzes each of the twenty-six Verdi operas in detail, inevitably leaving many readers frustrated by their inability to see live productions of all (though at least they can now be found on video, even the much-maligned *Alzira*, about the Incas in Peru).

Wealthy in old age, in 1896 Verdi endowed the construction of the Casa di Riposo per Musicisti (literally the "Rest Home for Musicians") for retired opera singers and musicians in Milan. It was designed in the neo-Gothic style, and both Verdi and his wife, Giuseppina Strepponi, are buried there. In the last years of his life, Verdi wrote to his friend Giulio Monteverde: "Of all my works, that which pleases me the most is the Casa that I had built in Milan to shelter elderly singers who have not been favoured by fortune, or who when they were young did not have the virtue of saving their money. Poor and dear companions of my life!"

Happy birthday, Giuseppe!

October 10, 2021

74

Wagnerism and the Fandom of the Opera

Periodic references to the works of composer Richard Wagner surface amid the florid descriptive prose of Marcel Proust, who associated the world views of his fictional characters with those of Wagner's operas and reflected on the emotional baggage shared by both listeners of music and readers of his works.

But Proust was not the only one to identify with elements of Wagner's rich operatic works, nor was this enthusiasm exclusive to audiences in nineteenth-century France. Even after 120 years it may still be observed in Wagnerophiles around the world, some travelling intercontinentally from one production of the *Ring* cycle tetralogy to another. From Seattle to Sydney, Buenos Aires to Beijing, Wagner fans attend performances, comparing Wotans, Norns, and the rest — genuine fandoms of the opera.

Essentially a timeless fairy tale for adults, the *Ring* cycle lends itself to updated interpretations, unlike Puccini's *Tosca* or Poulenc's *Dialogues of the Carmelites*, whose plots and actions are keyed to actual historical events. One of the more bizarre adaptations, dubbed "Eurotrash" by purists, placed the story on a spaceship. But one can also think of the "twilight of the gods," with the flooding of the Rhine below the burning of Valhalla, as a metaphor for global warming, which sounds less outlandish, and indeed has a hint of reality. While visual adherence to the original text may not be strictly essential, no substitution is allowed for its musical composition or performance; for example, a production could not substitute synthesizers for the Wagner tubas or drum kits for the Nibelung anvils. Wagner's sacrosanct music remains unaltered, whatever the peculiarities of the staging.

Music critic Alex Ross's recent book *Wagnerism* is not specifically devoted to the life of the composer himself, but is an examination of his political and racial views and their legacy and influence in Germany and elsewhere. Wagnerophiles in the early twentieth century notably included many within the Third Reich, who were said by novelist Thomas Mann and other exiles to have betrayed the "trusty and true guardians of the real Germany" with their sordid utilization of Wagner's magnificent music in their racist propaganda. Wagner's widow upon his death in 1883, Cosima, was an ardent Nazi who lived until the 1930s. She entertained Adolf Hilter and other Nazis at the Wagner home in Bavaria, where the operas were performed at annual festivals in Bayreuth (they continue to be presented there, in the theatre designed for them by her husband).

The use of Wagnerian motifs in cinema, such as the use of the "Ride of the Valkyries" from the *Ring* cycle in both D.W. Griffith's *Birth of a Nation* and Francis Ford Coppola's *Apocalypse Now,* illustrates how Wagnerism remains embedded in popular culture, remote from nineteenth-century Germany, extending beyond mere musical pleasure into the very texture of society itself. Even in the austere realm of Hermann Minkowski's four-dimensional concept of space-time, we can find lurking old Gurnemanz, knight of the Holy Grail from *Parsifal,* solemnly intoning, "Here time becomes space."

Wagnerism has penetrated deeply into many layers of thought, not only in tone but also in text, for he was his own librettist. In the twenty-first century his operas continue to create worshipful bourgeois fandoms.

April 25, 2021

75

Darwin, Wagner, an Earworm and Two Beagles

Charles Darwin's description of the circumnavigation of the globe as a young scientist in the years 1831 to 1836 in the *Voyage of the Beagle* is a fascinating account of his observations of plants, animals and geological formations, those that eventually led to his conception of evolution, heralding a new insight into biological science. In the summer of 1956, I read the account of Darwin's travels in Patagonia in my dog-eared paperback copy while travelling around Argentina, myself between periods of work in observational astronomy. Hoping to follow in Darwin's footsteps across the Andes, I boarded the electrified Transandine Railway in Mendoza, detraining at Las Cuevas, the last station on the Argentine side before the railway crosses into Chile.

Hiking up to the pass above the village, nestled between the peaks of Aconcagua (6,962 metres) to the north and Tupungato (6,570 metres) to the south, I sat in the thin air (at an elevation of about 3,810 metres) upon a rock below the huge statue *The Christ of the Andes* (allegedly facing east, according to the Chilenos, because "even the Son of God didn't dare turn His back on the Argentines"). Darwin, too, described the Uspallata Pass in his journal. In Chapter 25, "Passage of the Cordillera," he writes:

> The wind on the summit was exceedingly cold, but it was impossible not to stop for a few minutes to admire, again and again, the colour of the heavens, and the brilliant transparency of the atmosphere. The scenery was grand: to the westward there was a fine chaos of mountains, divided by profound ravines … .

Sitting at the same summit, I reread Darwin's description, feasting my eyes on the surrounding splendour, unexpectedly accompanied by an expansive earworm of "Siegfried's Journey to the Rhine" from Wagner's *Götterdämmerung*. When I'd earlier visited the Argentinian philosopher of science Mario Bunge in Buenos Aires, he had given me a recording of the opera, my first encounter with the music of Wagner. Later based at McGill University in Montreal, Bunge had a notable career as a scientist and philosopher. We never met again, and he died earlier this year, aged 100. Darwin did well too.

Since that time over a half century ago, whenever I hear that orchestral excerpt, whether recorded or live in Seattle or Berlin, an image is conjured between my ears of Darwin and me at the same spot, both transfixed by the display of grandeur from the Uspallata Pass beneath the great Aconcagua and Tupungato, both of us twenty-two years old, but separated from one another by an interval of over 120 years.

When we are all gone, the Andes will still be there. Meanwhile there is the Beagle Public House in Cook St. Village, Victoria, British Columbia, where, when asked about the name, the bartender told me the name was of the breed of dog, not the sailing ship that took Darwin around the world as a young man, setting him on his course of thinking about nature and the descent of species.

Darwin later wrote in 1859, "There is grandeur in this view of life … . From so simple a beginning endless forms most beautiful and most wonderful have been, and are being, evolved."

November 29, 2020; revised October 30, 2021

76

Quests

Narratives of searching for a valued object or sacred goal have been a common genre in myth and legend, and at times even in the world of everyday life and scientific research. Jason and his Argonauts sought the golden fleece, medieval knights the Holy Grail and contemporary physicists the Higgs boson (quantum theory having correctly predicted the latter, though proven at enormous expense with the construction of high-energy particle colliders). A search may also be for an abstract idea, such as the quasi-metaphysical quest for the "true essence of meaning," which engaged the attention of analytical philosophers in the last century and became an ideological bone of contention among them.

While a student at the University of Minnesota in 1954, I once stopped attending a seminar in epistemology led by the eminent American philosopher Wilfrid Sellars, finding it dull after the first session. Ten years later Sellars returned to the university as a visiting lecturer, presenting a forty-five-minute talk to an audience of colleagues and students. I attended, being then more mature, hoping to this time appreciate hearing what he had to say. Regrettably, the early afternoon lecture followed a substantial luncheon, with the effect of provoking naps in the stuffy overheated auditorium. Within a few minutes of the start of his presentation, I nodded off and only awakened as he raised his voice in his concluding summary, screwing up his piggy little eyes and booming out the profound conclusion, "And *that* is the true essence of meaning!"

In this moment, I reaffirmed my desire to *not* pursue an advanced degree in philosophy. Instead, I would stick to science, leaving interpretations of the essence of meaning (whatever that was) to professional academic philosophers, myself sharing the earthier opinion of R. Crumb's Mr. Natural: "Don't mean shee-it!"

The goal in science of understanding natural phenomena is a more serious business than speculative metaphysics, but there are still golden fleeces and holy grails in our quests. The elaboration of a combined unifying theory of both relativity and quantum mechanics remains an elusive goal. Each explains certain observed phenomena effectively, but combining them remains tantalizingly elusive. Quantum gravity and the bidirectional aspect of time, among other issues, remain enigmatic goals of ongoing and future quests.

June 2, 2021

77

The Hero

After penning a couple of dozen bestselling thrillers featuring the American ex-army policeman Jack Reacher, English author Lee Child has now taken up non-fiction and literary criticism. His recent extended essay *The Hero* considers the origin and role of the fictional concept, starting with presumed stone-age storytelling, continuing through Homer and evolving through history to the present day. Child seems QBE (qualified by experience) to have chosen this subject for his consideration, having previously been employed in the entertainment industry and knowledgeable about what sells. His essay was published recently by the *Times Literary Supplement* as a compact 77-page hardcover book.

Presenting Odysseus as an example, Child explains how the term *hero* "meant, in practice, one who suffers, and endures, and survives a long and complicated journey through dangers and perils, in order to do good in some vague and unspecified way." He identifies three ways of using the word: in literary analysis, as a political hook by rulers and as a main character in a book or popular story, such as that of Robin Hood (whose character was invented and refined over many years, giving to fiction what wasn't found in real life — there being no historical person called Robin Hood.) The hero concept resurfaced again and again, clearly seen in the exploits of the contrived fictional hero James Bond during the Cold War in the last century.

Even Child's hero fits neatly into the scheme: Jack Reacher is a contemporary knight errant rescuing maidens (and others) in danger, then moving on after slaying the "dragons" of evil gangsters, crooked businessmen and politicians, and fiendish cult leaders. The elaborate plots and the repeated similar adventures of Child's knight errant hero effectively capture the imagination of readers in his page-turners, invariably terminating in a happy conclusion, though Reacher always leaves the rescued damsel and moves on.

The concept of the knight errant, elaborated in great detail by Johan Huizinga in his account of the late Middle Ages, arose in the spiritual orders of knighthood around the time of the crusades. Such a knight was poor and free of ties to any lord or ruler. Of course, the ideal of a noble and unencumbered warrior remains today a cultural icon in many guises, from cowboys to spacemen. Huizinga also identifies an erotic undertone to the knight errant, writing, "Every sixteen-year-old male [yearns] to display his courage before a woman, expose himself to dangers and to be strong … as the young hero who liberates the virgin. Even if the enemy occasionally is an unsuspecting dragon, the sexual element remains just below the surface."

In journalism the terms *hero* and *heroine* are employed to refer to those employed in potentially dangerous occupations at times when ordinary members of the public are threatened, as with health care workers in these times of viral pandemic. These individuals may be selfless, noble and deserving of praise, but they are not knights errant in the sense described by authors Child or Huizinga in their books.

May 25, 2021

78

Kullervo

The nineteenth-century Romantic composer Felix Mendelssohn wrote a series of short lyrical piano pieces called *Songs Without Words* between 1829 and 1845 that remain popular today among pianists after nearly 200 years.

"Words without songs," however, may be said to describe the influence of the story of the tragic hero Kullervo, who first became known at the same time as Felix Mendelssohn's compositions. His story, however, was originally sung by Finnish bards in Karelia, that once-remote corner of northeastern Europe now comprising eastern Finland and an area of northwestern Russia, a land of dense forests with wolves and bears, once populated by an illiterate peasantry speaking a non-Indo-European dialect that was later incorporated into the standard Finnish language.

Tales from this area were collected by the physician and philologist Elias Lönnrot in the second quarter of the nineteenth century and published as the *Kalevala*, which became widely influential in Finnish culture, including visual art, music and literary works. The story of Kullervo from Lönnrot's collection inspired works by, among others, dramatist Aleksis Kivi, painter Akseli Gallen-Kallela and composer Jean Sibelius, whose first major success was a symphonic cantata built from scenes of the work. More recently, the Finnish composer Aulis Sallinen created an opera based on the story, an angular and harsh work filled with explosions of rage by outbursts of tympani and other startling percussive effects.

English author J.R.R. Tolkien also wrote an early unfinished short story about Kullervo in 1915–16, recently published along with essays and commentary about his wonder at having discovered the pagan world of *Kalevala* as a youth, describing it as analogous to John Keats's 1816 work "On First Looking into Chapman's Homer," with "stout Cortez" "silent, upon a peak in Darien" seeing the Pacific Ocean for the first time.

The story of Kullervo is of an orphaned and unnurtured youth, Kullervo, who becomes a slave when sold by a guardian due to his incompetent work. Kullervo later seduces his new master's wife, though he kills her when she mocks him for being a slave. When he eventually finds his surviving parents, they abandon him upon learning he is a murderer. He has sex with a maiden who turns out to be his long-lost sister, and she then kills herself from shame upon realizing who he is. Kullervo's horror leads him to curse his own existence and then to commit suicide by falling on his sword.

This powerful tale of a hero — or better, anti-hero — remains relevant today, for Kullervo's life story encapsulates the human propensity to retain the ancient reptilian portion of our brains, which, when uncontrolled, leads to destructive behaviour. We all have our inner Raskolnikovs and Kullervos and are capable of both coldly calculated murder and spontaneous episodes of wrath and rage. This potential likely can never be eliminated, for it is part of who we are as a species. But hopefully we may at least be attenuated by what Kullervo lacked, as was recognized by the narrator in the *Kalevala*: parental guidance and early childhood education. These words, chanted without music, tell of the ultimate fate of a child deprived of love and affection.

December 1, 2021

79

Grid Poetry in the Carolingian Renaissance

Charlemagne (c. 743–781) is known to have been a promoter of medieval education, ushering in a rebirth of learning after the decay of classicism with the fall of the Roman Empire. This renaissance, however, was mired in suffocating Christian religiosity and limited to a few specific monasterial centres scattered about the otherwise universal illiteracy of the European population at the time, like bright stars shining in front of a cloud of dark matter, quite unlike the greater renaissance of the eleventh century, which saw the rise of universities and general cultural awakening.

Charlemagne's government patronized a variety of activities that together produced a form of cultural renewal, whose prime goal was the extension and improvement of Latin literacy. Achieving this goal required the production of books containing the essentials of Christian Latin culture. In the absence of printing, these books were all written and transcribed by hand in various monastic milieux.

Hrabanus Maurus (c. 780–856) was one such scholar. Elected Archbishop of Mainz in 847 and considered a founder of the literary German language, he produced a unique classical genre of poetry consisting of a grid of letters overlaid by images illustrating the words and sentiments concealed within them. His most famous work in this form was a series of twenty-eight poems dedicated to the Christian image of the cross. Composed around 810–814, it contained not only references to scripture in the imagery but also to numerology, arising from associations of both natural and theological concepts with integers.

For example, in totalling 28, the quantity of poems reflects a "perfect number," 28 being the sum of its divisors (1, 2, 4, 7 and 14). But the number 28 may also represent the total of 24 books of the *Hebrew Bible* plus the 4 Gospels. Many of the poems offer a meditation involving some combination of theological and numerological significance, a fascinating idea of relating two different abstract systems, one of Christian theology, the other of pure mathematics.

This impressive collection of grid poetry has been preserved in various European centres and is reproduced with full-page colour illustrations in Eliot Weinberger's book *Angels and Saints*, each poem explained in detail by medieval scholar and historian Mary Wellesley. They provide an erudite finishing touch to Weinberger's unique reflections on angels and saints and his parable of the afterlife, inviting readers to reflect on this concept, arising from their own world views.

April 20, 2021

80

Of Montaigne

Michel Eyquem de Montaigne (1533–1592) was one of the most significant authors of the French Renaissance, nearly 500 years ago, credited with creating and popularizing the essay as a literary genre. His collected works, *Essais*, have influenced many, mainly European, writers and thinkers for nearly half a millennium.

To summarize Montaigne's thinking, which was mostly self-referential, is undeniably a challenging task, and English writer Sarah Bakewell made a good stab at it in 2010 with her book *How to Live: A Life of Montaigne in One Question and Twenty Attempts at an Answer.*

I read Bakewell's work when it was first published, and as a writer of essays myself, I appreciated the work Bakewell had done to integrate Montaigne's life and works in a form readily accessible to an intelligent reader.

Often characterized as a philosopher, Montaigne's astute reflections from those early years of printing aren't really a system of philosophy, but simply the honest thoughts of a wealthy and educated man of his times. The new technology of printing allowed him to disseminate these thoughts to others, and perhaps he even had this in mind while writing. His serious ruminations on the vicissitudes of life and death, and other timeless reflections, were relevant not only to the age of the French Renaissance but to all ages since.

Montaigne's essays influenced many later thinkers, including Blaise Pascal, who, despite admiring religious zealotry, quite unlike Montaigne's negative opinion thereof, liked his style of writing. Voltaire waded in, defending Montaigne's rejection of extremism of belief in religion. Nietzsche claimed that the very existence of Montaigne's *Essays* added to the joy of living in the world, and more recently, Montaigne was cited as a precursor of Freud, using free association to cure mental illness.

Bakewell's book is structured into twenty chapters, each encapsulating the question, "How to live?" with specific recommendations from Montaigne, such as not worrying about death, paying attention to one's surroundings, surviving love and loss, being skeptical and convivial, seeing the world, and the desire to reflect on everything and regret nothing, to give up control, and to be ordinary and imperfect. In sum, the desire to simply allow one's life to be its own justification.

Each chapter of Bakewell's work also relates episodes of Montaigne's life: his living situation, his occupation as the owner of his family's estate and as a municipal politician, his friends and family, and the unstable society of sixteenth-century France, with its raging religious wars and terrible atrocities. Much of what Montaigne experienced in his era resonates with the human struggles to survive in our own times.

His style of writing no doubt influenced my own, when in later years I shifted from writing clinical reports and academic papers to simply describing what I found interesting in the world around me, as I experienced it.

October 9, 2021

81

Edward Gorey and Marcel Proust

Writing in the *London Review of Books,* Rosemary Hill recently reviewed a biography of the eccentric American writer and illustrator Edward Gorey: *Born to be Posthumous* by Mark Dery. Dery's work is a fascinating and comprehensive account of Gorey's life and works and contains two brief summaries of Gorey's bizarre short and enigmatic graphic tales, including *The Doubtful Guest* (1957).

Dery describes Gorey's "guest" as a creature

> something between a penguin and a lizard, smaller than anyone in the family, … [with] a peculiar appearance, [who] … does not understand language. As time passes it becomes greedy and destructive [and] … has temper tantrums …, yet nobody even tries to get rid of it; their attitude toward it remains one of resigned acceptance…. After about seventeen years most children leave home.

But the guest remained.

This peculiar story came to my mind while reading Marcel Proust's long novel about the search for lost time. As Proust's asthmatic and obsessive narrator muses, "an unwanted guest for luncheon deprives us from solitude without offering us company." The two images of a doubtful and unwanted guest merge to offer a picture of both annoyance and indecision that is never resolved. I wondered whether others had noticed this similarity between the two literary works.

The awkward social situation described by both Proust and Gorey called for further investigation. A web search revealed that answering lists of questions to illuminate one's ambitions was, in fact, a popular pastime in the nineteenth century. Now called the Proust questionnaire, it consisted of a list of questions meant to reveal aspects of the subject's personality. As a teen in 1890, Proust wrote out answers to one such English questionnaire, his written answers later discovered in the 1920s. The Proust questionnaire has continued to amuse and instruct ever since.

Gorey himself was asked to take the questionnaire for *Vanity Fair* magazine, and his answers were printed in the October 1997 issue (later compiled and published in an online blog by Edward Gorey fan Irwin Terry at goreyana.blogspot.com). Gorey's answers are typically enigmatic:

What is your current state of mind? "Changeable."
Which living person do you most despise? "Where to begin ...?"
What is your most marked characteristic? "Dither."

I remain unaware if Gorey had any opinion of Proust himself, but the questionnaire sounds like fun for a party game.

June 24, 2021

82

Reproustification

Proustification is the effect upon a reader or writer of becoming entranced by the florid prose of Marcel Proust, whose novel *In Search of Lost Time* presents a challenge to the reader not only of sheer length but also of imagery — a cascade of similes and metaphors, a veritable Niagara of words, drenching the pages and inundating the senses of his readers.

The heroic length of Proust's novel and the sheer density of the text may present such a challenge to the aspiring young writer that it inhibits their own composition. Virginia Woolf once described her feelings of ineptness as a developing author after encountering Proust early on, writing, "My great adventure is really Proust. Well — what remains to be written after that?" Woolf was evidently able to set aside her feelings of awe about the novel and go on to write her own masterpieces, although eventually she was weighted down by irremediable ennui and felt compelled to check out — but that's another story.

My first exposure to serious fiction was as an undergraduate student of humanities, when I first read (and then reread) Tolstoy's *War and Peace* and the Dostoevsky classics *Crime and Punishment* and *The Brothers Karamazov*. Later, though, I concentrated on physical and biological science and public health. But after qualifying in psychiatry, I was drawn back into the world of humanity and began to read fiction again after retiring from the pressure of being a hospital consultant. I had heard of Proust and began reading *In Search of Lost Time,* but becoming bogged down in the verbiage, I gave it up after the first volume.

Over the years, I became more familiar with what critics and other writers were saying about Proust. Involuntarily confined, like Montaigne, to my tower by social distancing, I resolved to give it another try, reading it in ten- to fifteen-minute intervals while riding a stationary exercise bike given to me by my boyfriend. It took me eleven months to complete all seven volumes, simultaneously exercising both mind and body.

I became, as it were, reproustified by immersion, enchanted by the prose.

January 26, 2021

83

Camus and COVID

Since the start of the pandemic in the (northern) winter of 2020, bookshops reported that newly reprinted copies of Albert Camus's 1947 novel *The Plague* have been flying off the shelves, though the illness depicted in the novel was bacterial, not viral, and spread by vectors of rats and fleas instead of inhaled viral aerosol droplets infecting the nasal passages.

What is common to the two communicable diseases, though, are the human reactions to the mortal threat inherent in them. We are all, so to speak, at death's door (some of us closer than others), and the issue of our eventual nonexistence is seldom a source of immediate concern. Yet living in the midst of a worldwide pandemic of potentially lethal infection tends to draw attention to what is usually suppressed.

Like all of us, the characters in Camus's novel display different modes of psychological adjustment to their sudden threat. The main protagonist, Dr. Rieux, is depicted as soldiering on, treating and consoling those mortally ill to the best of his ability and training. Another keeps a diary and organizes a team of volunteers, later dying himself of the disease. A journalist, who initially tries to arrange an escape from the locked-down city, comes to feel guilt and chooses to remain and fight. A mentally unstable individual attempts to hang himself and is rescued, though he loses control and becomes disorganized in thought and behaviour. A priest, who initially attributes the plague to human sin, as was the case historically, later softens his tone and accepts the need to support the group of volunteers. And a medical colleague of Dr. Rieux works to make an antidote serum while a senior medical official initially downplays the severity of the illness so as not to "alarm the public."

The wide range of human responses to the plague displayed in Camus's novel may also be seen in today's pandemic, and the philosophical reflections about life and death remain timely. In summing up, Camus's narrator concludes with the celebrated quotation, "There is more to admire than to despise among human beings."

July 20, 2021

84

Translation

To perfectly translate or move a text across from one language to another is not possible, but usually one can approximate the content and, with more difficulty, the aura of the original. In the afterword to his 2018 English translation of the great 1929 German novel *Berlin Alexanderplatz* by Berlin physician Alfred Döblin, Michael Hofmann sagely wrote, "A translation is, after all, an imitation, a performance, a substitution."

The German original of *Berlin Alexanderplatz* is replete with Berliner slang from the last days of the doomed Weimar Republic, presenting the translator with the nearly impossible challenge of replicating expressions resistant to alteration by those unfamiliar with the colours, conflicts, sounds and smells of a society different from, yet not entirely dissimilar to, their own. The novel portrays characters in a German culture plunging towards extinction, culminating in 1933, the year of my birth, when Hitler became dictator. The Weimar Republic was a decadent society, and the story of its demise is relevant to the times in which we live, doomed not only by the ongoing political and economic upheavals, but also by the now unstoppable environmental catastrophe.

As a more humorous example, when translating a Finnish murder mystery into English a few years ago as an exercise when studying that non-Indo-European language, I was stymied by not understanding a conversation between two Helsinki gangsters. Alluding to a third, they said he had once "turned the crank on a ski lift." My tutor enlightened me: the allusion was to jerking off, masturbation.

"False friends" are also a snag for the unaware translator, in both spoken as well as written language. I remember once asking for *sopa* (soup) instead of *jabón* (soap) at a hotel in Argentina when still learning Spanish, and another time hearing an American lady at a café there asking a waiter for a bidet, when she wanted the popular soft drink Bidú.

A unique form of translation can be seen in the popular writings of scientists trying to explain in non-technical language their theoretical work in fields like physics and cosmology. They converse effectively with their colleagues about quantum theory and the dimensions of space and time using mathematical jargon, but use analogies ranging from dead cats to universal extinction for those of us not trained in their specialties.

As one's familiarity with different languages expands, the possibility of interlingual homophony and puns increases, as when a sudden gust of wind elevated the skirt of a female passenger on the Parisian metro and a local resident commented in French, "*C'est la vie*" (such is life) to his seatmate from Spain, who replied in Spanish, "*Se la vi tambien, pero no dijo nada*" (I saw it too but didn't say anything).

July 13, 2021

85

Conventional Signage

Charles Dodgson (a.k.a. Lewis Carroll), the nineteenth-century English mathematician, logician and author of children's literature, wrote in his famous, bizarre nonsense poem *The Hunting of the Snark*, as lines declaimed by the bellman (captain) of a ship when showing his crew a blank navigation chart:

> "What's the good of Mercator's North Poles
> and Equators
> Tropics, Zones, and Meridian Lines?"
> So the bellman would cry: and the crew would reply
> "They are merely conventional signs!

A unique moment in time may be represented by a word acting as a conventional sign, like formerly designating a year as BC (before Christ) or AD (*anno Domini*), or nowadays the neutral BCE (before the common era) and CE (common era). As a professor of symbolic logic at Oxford, Dodgson knew all about signs, conventional and otherwise. In the twentieth century his great and tragic successor Kurt Gödel devised a system of signs, representing both mathematical and logical symbols, as a means of proving theorems about abstract quantities.

Thinking about conventional signs today, the last day of the year 2021, the fact that we celebrate changing calendars tonight is but another conventional sign, based on custom, not an astronomical event like an equinox or solstice. In most English-speaking countries, the last day of December is known as New Year's Eve and is celebrated socially as a festival of change and with hope of a better future in the coming year. In Scotland, however, December 31 is called Hogmanay and is celebrated in massive crowds as people gather in torchlight parades, participants hugging one another, suffused in the fumes of the traditional beverage of Scotland while singing "Auld Lang Syne." Translated literally, the title of the song means "old long since," but the meaning is more like "old times" or "the olden days," the song being a farewell to past times, and marking the unique point in calendar time of transition to the following year.

It will be a bleak day today in Scotland, however, for Hogmanay has been officially cancelled due to the need to maintain social distancing in the COVID pandemic. At least there should be fewer hangovers on the morning of January 1, 2022, in that part of the UK.

December 31, 2021

86

Erotic Writings

From ancient times, sexually explicit images and printed matter have been consumed by viewers worldwide of all ages and erotic dispositions. "Something for everybody" is literally true; "whatever turns your crank," as is said in Finnish. Some governments attempt to control access to such printed or digitally shared material, with possession prohibited to greater or lesser degrees depending on imagery and age of subjects portrayed.

Countries with an Abrahamic religious heritage often tend to have the harshest restrictions, particularly in English-speaking jurisdictions, or in those that are remnants of British colonialism, with social mores reflecting those of the colonizer rather than the colonized. On the whole, those countries with a legal background derived from the Napoleonic Code, which omits describing offences pertaining to private sexual conduct, tend to be more lenient, though material with prepubertal child subjects is usually forbidden, considered exploitative, and scenes other than ordinary heterosexual sex play are sometimes restricted because of homophobia in the forbidders.

Arguments for the restriction of pornography often invoke pseudoscientific ideas about what is and is not "natural" regarding sexual behaviour in their efforts to control viewing, often only reflecting values of biblical origin found in the Book of Leviticus in the *Tanakh* (the Jewish bible) and the letters of St. Paul in the Christian *New Testament*. Sexologists today assert that all human sexual behaviour is natural.

From a medical and psychiatric view there is no evidence that self-stimulation to orgasm associated with viewing pornography has any negative effect on physical or mental health; indeed, it may be useful for many reasons, like assuaging sexual frustration among those who are unable to enjoy mutual relief with a partner due to age, disability, institutional confinement or shyness. I have testified on this opinion in a submission to the Canadian Border Services Agency at their request in 1994.

Literary erotic writing of sexual behaviour, as seen in the poetical *Song of Songs* in the *Hebrew Bible*, is accepted as canonical because of its alleged authorship by Solomon and its basis as an allegorical interpretation, the subject matter being taken as not sexual desire but rather God's love for Israel. Christian theology correspondingly regards it as a metaphorical relationship between God and the (Catholic) Church.

The extremely explicit love letters of James Joyce to his beloved partner Nora in the early twentieth century were fiercely denounced by governments in Ireland and the UK when the contents were revealed after publication in the *Paris Review* (https://www.theparisreview. org/blog/2018/02/02/james-joyces-love-letters-dirty-little-fuckbird/).

Since sexual expression is genetically coded into human beings as a necessary factor to preserve the species by means of sexual reproduction, there is little success in trying to control it by religious and civil authorities, and try as they might to prevent its expression, such efforts are usually foiled by nature having its way.

October 25, 2020; revised October 5, 2021, and March 15, 2022

87

Burning the Books

Oxford chief librarian Richard Ovenden's new book about the loss of libraries and archives by different destructive events, titled *Burning the Books*, was recently reviewed in the *Times Literary Supplement* by James Waddell. Among the causes of loss described by Ovenden are fire, war, neglect and, most significantly in the twenty-first century, "the abundance and transience of digital information."

Perhaps the most infamous, purposeful mass burning of books is the May 10, 1933, Nazi bonfire on Opernplatz in Berlin. Today, a unique and emotionally powerful memorial now adorns the site of the book-burning in Berlin. Set below ground and viewable from street level through a transparent thick glass window are rows upon rows of empty shelves. Nothing more demarcates their destruction, aside from a plaque on the ground describing the event that took place there eighty-eight years previously. When I visited the site in 1999, there was a teacher explaining its history to a group of secondary school students. In the nearby Humboldt University bookstall across the Unter den Linden boulevard, I bought a copy of Erich Maria Remarque's 1928 anti-war book *Im Westen nichts Neues* (*All Quiet on the Western Front*) that, unlike almost all other copies, somehow had survived the burning.

While today it is relatively easy to upload books and archival information, as the collapse of civilization ensues from wars and other forms of discontent associated with the destruction of our planetary environment, it is reasonable to wonder whether digitally coded records will survive as the computer age descends with us into the hell of xenophobic violence, religious superstition and the deliberate destruction of books and documents by those with the power to do so, as was done on that fateful day in May 1933.

Looking ahead to the end of the century and beyond, it's hard to imagine digitization surviving the coming social collapse, perhaps not failing immediately but surely disappearing over eons, for any future archaeologists to unearth and decode. Having no illusions about the permanence of these essays in an online blog format, I also make printed copies, which may survive a few decades or centuries longer but, like everything else, will eventually rot, leaving nothing behind but "footprints in the slime of time."

June 6, 2021

TIME PAST

88

Time, and Time Again

Marcel Proust, author of the early twentieth-century French novel *In Search of Lost Time* (also translated as *Remembrance of Things Past*) was no superficial slouch when it came to commenting on Albert Einstein's relativistic portrayal of time as associated with the three dimensions of space. Among a torrent of insights, such as "We may sometimes find a person again, but we cannot abolish time" in Volume 6, Proust wrote, "Distances are only the relation of space to time, and vary with that relation."

Later in life, Einstein reflected, "The distinction between past, present, and future is only a stubborn persistent illusion." While the idea of a timeless, predetermined view of reality is now generally accepted, having been predicted and verified by general relativity in observational astronomy and in the laws of motion, there is still a significant conceptual problem regarding the idea of time-lessness found within quantum mechanics, which describes with great accuracy the properties of matter at the micro scale, where irreversible changes are observed that definitively distinguish the past from the future, as in the phenomenon of radioactive decay or the nuclear fusion within stars that forms new elements. These changes, though observable, are unpredictable, except in terms of probability among a group of particles, but the probability of being someplace is a mathematical construct, and not the same thing as specifying the position of a particle in space.

The difficulty inherent in only probabilistic estimates may be avoided, suggests Swiss physicist Nicolas Gisin, by employing a tool known as *intuitionist mathematics*. Gisin's recent publications have stimulated discussion of this approach among particle physicists. Intuitionist mathematics differs from the usual representation of the number system in that it indicates real numbers with infinite digits along a continuum approximating a digit that cannot be exactly measured, like making 0.9999 equal to 1.0.

Mathematical languages themselves shape our understanding of time in physics, for what we have been calling "real numbers" are themselves not any more real than are unicorns; their reality is one of our imaginations, not a feature of nature. Yet the words *real* and *imaginary* seem inappropriate for describing number systems, and it might be less confusing to call them something simpler, like saying *type 1* instead of *real* and *type 2* instead of *imaginary*. Number systems, after all, are abstract entities, not concrete objects.

But clarifying the terminology doesn't help in trying to account for Einstein's "illusion" of the flow of time. As Galileo responded to the demands of the Holy Inquisition to deny heliocentricity, "*E pur si muove*" (It moves anyway).

August 15, 2021

89

Summarizing Proust

Marcel Proust wrote about time as memories, perhaps like a fluid in which life events are immersed. But when we direct our attention away from what transpires in the vicissitudes of daily life to the universe in which we are embedded, with dimensions of space as well as time, we lift our eyes away from human affairs to consider where, as well as when, events occur.

Challenged in 1972 by a professor of anatomy to explain what medicine had to do with astronomy, I suggested somewhat flippantly that coincidentally, the founder of modern anatomy, Vesalius, and the founder of new heliocentric cosmology, Copernicus, had both published their works in the same year — 1543. Now half a century later, a similar question arises in considering the possible relationship between cosmology and neurobiology, in that both the architecture of time and space of the former and the complex connections among brain nerve cells in the latter occupy the outer limits of our understanding of astronomy and biology.

We are fascinated by the extremes revealed in the great and tiny, from clusters of remote galaxies in expanding space to DNA in living systems and quarks combining to form subatomic particles. In her book *The End of Everything,* cosmologist Katie Mack reflects on the possible end states of the universe, and theoretical physicist Jeremy England, in his book *Every Life on Fire,* writes about the possible transition between inert matter and living systems. Both authors are specialists in their chosen scientific fields, and while they speculate about possible consequences of their hypotheses, what they have in common is the underlying assumption of empirical observation being the only appropriate method of understanding nature.

Isaiah Berlin's metaphor of the hedgehog and the fox seems relevant to reflections about cosmology and biology, for while it may take a hedgehog a lifetime to attain real expertise in either, a fox, once familiar with how they may relate to one another, what they may have in common as representations of the natural world, and how they differ, and how these affect us, reveals a link between the great and the small of the universe within which we find ourselves.

Quantum field theory and thermodynamics may be complicated, yet they are more understandable than human behaviour. Proust considered these things a century ago, writing in Chapter 1 of Book 5 of *In Search of Lost Time*, "The stellar universe is not so difficult to comprehend as the real actions of other people."

This may be only a fifteen-second summary of the novel, but it will do.

June 6, 2021

90

Wrinkled Surfaces and Saving Time

In *In Search of Lost Time,* Marcel Proust observed that the journey from Paris to Normandy may be best accomplished by motorcar, since it is thought by some to be a more authentic way to travel, "following more nearly, in a closer intimacy, the various contours by which the surface of the earth is wrinkled." Proust compares this alternative mode of transportation to travelling by train, in which one is whisked through a cut or along an embankment, always on as level a grade as possible, flying across chasms, plunging through tunnels blasted into the immovable mountainous wrinkles of the Earth's surface, all to maintain a fast speed and, supposedly, "save time."

One can prolong a journey by decreasing speed, travelling by bicycle or by foot, perhaps even becoming immersed in the panorama itself by ascending a mountain to experience the view, though some would consider this a "waste of time." Yet accepting the personal challenge of such an ascent rewards the climber with the sight of what is denied those who remain in the valleys. The metaphor of climbing is also appropriate to the process of education or learning, whether leading to an academic degree or merely contributing to the knowledge of the student, and by doing so, denying the accusation of "wasting time."

Like money, time can be spent and wasted, but unlike money, never saved. It can be invested in work, play, amusement or education, for those that have the opportunity and inclination, but for most humans, time is probably simply spent in distraction or survival.

Beyond these goals, most people attempt to prolong life, hurriedly seeking opportunities to facilitate this wish, creating the illusion of using speed to "save time." But speed itself is constrained by both time and gravity, as are we ourselves, our bodies sagging and drooping as we speed towards our final destination. Yet we may be capable of delaying oblivion by maintaining some degree of physical fitness, such as by solitary pedalling of an exercise bike, going nowhere but reading Proust on an electronic device, savouring the florid prose, conjuring up an experience of travel no longer accessible to the reader.

Reading Proust is like climbing a mountain, not of wrinkles in the surface of the Earth, but of a narrative of florid prose, displaying psychological vistas unseen by those who limit themselves to less than 280 words.

February 25, 2021

91

An Unattainable Destination

Having read many of the Jan Morris travel accounts (and having even reviewed one of them, *Manhattan 45*), I was delighted in 1985 to acquire her latest book at the time, *Last Letters from Hav*, an enchanting and elaborate description of an extended visit to the fictional city state of Hav, an isolated peninsular city evoking comparison to maritime cities of the Eastern Mediterranean or Black Sea.

Hav is connected to Russia by a single nineteenth-century railway line penetrating a formidable escarpment, and Morris closely examines its colourful location and society during a several-month sojourn. She portrays with inimitable prose the quasi–Middle Eastern mixed ethnicity of Hav's inhabitants and the city's historical origins, religious affiliations, cultural traditions, sporting activities, cuisines, monuments and other unique attractions, making Hav appear a pleasant destination for any curious visitor with an interest in unusual and exotic locales.

I gave the book to my daughter, herself a well-travelled intercontinental entertainer, and, finding it again myself in a used bookshop on an island in the Salish Sea some twenty years later, I bought and decided to reread it. The expanded 2006 edition reprinted the original book as Part 1 and provided new material in Part 2, titled

Hav of the Myrmidons, a follow-up account of the author's return to the area for six days in 2005.

This second sojourn revealed a transformed society, no longer with quaint customs but remodelled into a money-making enterprise with modern conveniences and, among other things, an exclusive Club Med–type resort for wealthy tourists, everything updated and commercialized to a degree more appropriate to the twenty-first century. The city now boasted a freeway connecting residential districts instead of dirt tracks, a skyscraper and a shiny new airport, replacing the abandoned railway connection.

Who actually made the decision to modernize Hav is not directly specified by Morris, but she hints at it being a mysterious new religious authority bearing the Homeric name Myrmidons, with an intimated connection to China, which though not outwardly intrusive, evidently exerted sufficient thought control for their values to become accepted and internalized among those remaining in Hav since Morris's initial visit. But while Hav has become a clean and safe destination, it is now sanitized, appearing to have lost its soul, its former charm as an "exotic" destination, echoing changes sustained elsewhere, here in the real world.

A brilliant review of the second edition of *Hav* by Ursula Le Guin appeared in the *Guardian* in June 2006, reflecting on the losses imposed by time on one's memories of earlier adventures. An unavoidable consequence of living to an advanced age is having to retain images of places one loved when younger. Nostalgia becomes all the more poignant even when the loss, like Hav, is imaginary.

December 5, 2020

92

Unofficial Britain

Inspired by the detritus of the last century, Gareth E. Rees's new book *Unofficial Britain* reveals an image of a society founded in hope but now in the process of decay, with enduring structures haunted by memories and fears both real and imaginary, memories of "sensations rather than pictures" that provoke us to supply explanations that may or may not be real or even verifiable.

This beautifully crafted prose is no ordinary travelogue. Modestly subtitled *Journeys through Unexpected Places,* Rees's book limits his explorations to his own land, visiting and reflecting on what he perceives as "the magic, mythology and folklore of Urban Space," presenting an anthropological approach to the emotions and ideas arising from now empty factories, electricity pylons, ring roads and roundabouts, and other monuments constructed in the past century, some still in use, others abandoned.

As with twentieth-century Victorian creations like architectural "follies" — exotic temples constructed on private properties by wealthy landowners — Edwardians were fascinated by what some thought to be manifestations of the supernatural, and Victorians, reminiscing on past glories, had fantasies about haunted structures from earlier days. An imagined past persisted with mysteries and fears. Rees reflects, "The older I get the more I realize that the past is as unknowable as the future; it is just as prone to supposition and speculation."

The "unofficial Britain" of Rees may just be centred on the perception of the past as arising from impressions in the present. Yet today's present becomes tomorrow's past, as the Janus-faced moment of *now* constantly shifts into *then.* Rees exhibits a Proustian reflection on time past, not limited to Britain but colouring all human attempts to slow the merciless unfolding of the present. We are haunted by these reminders, from Celtic standing stones to the rusting steelworks of industry and the scars remaining from the extraction of minerals. Within cities, stately homes become tourist attractions and an abandoned power station an art gallery, but what will those survivors of the twenty-first century (if any) make of abandoned and seemingly haunted structures like disused airports or empty urban towers?

Future generations may find our own ghosts lurking in the structures we leave behind, as we transform the sad surface of our planet into a midden.

February 14, 2021

93

Ruins

A recent review in the *London Review of Books* examined two books about the architectural remains of a great metropolis, the capital of an intercontinental empire, to which it was said that all roads led. A city said to have been founded in 753 BCE, initially a kingdom, later a republic, a dictatorship and an empire, before finally becoming the centre of administrative offices for a formerly obscure Hebrew cult known as Christianity, which dominated Western culture for the following two millennia. Rome.

The Ruins Lesson: Meaning and Material in Western Culture by Susan Stewart describes how antiquarian artists in the early modern period focused on engravings, first in the sixteenth century, by examining two graphic artists from the Netherlands, Maarten van Heemskerck and Hieronymus Cock, who emphasized the decay and vegetative shrouding of ancient monumental structures, and later the eighteenth century, through the work of the Venetian classical archeologist Piranesi, who portrayed elaborate and baroque graphic fantasies of sites before the decline and fall of the empire.

Neatly complementing these pictorial representations is another work, devoted to cartographical locations within the ancient metropolis, *The Eternal City: A History of Rome in Maps*, compiled by Jessica Maier. Maier considered the ancient city by examining works by artists and mapmakers over the centuries, assembling the visual material into a compound picture. Many attempts have been made to visualize the layout of these ancient structures, some now removed or replaced, with imagined views of the city from the seven hills of the metropolis below them. Contemporary exercises in imagination, perhaps, but whose authenticity is probably better than simple guesswork.

Both Stewart's and Maier's works induce reflection on the future of humanity, beyond present understanding of the past of these and other ancient ruins worldwide. Our commercial and residential towers, sports stadiums, infrastructures in concrete of highways and railways may seem permanent emblems of our civilization, but this sense of permanence is as illusory as was that of ancient Rome. Two millennia hence, what of ours will endure?

Who will be the Gibbons to explain our decline and fall? How will the archaeologists of the future, if any, picture our ruins and map our Manhattans, Londons and Shanghais? Will indeed *anything* remain after we are gone, as the sea waters rise and our Walhallas burn, is this the twilight of *our* gods?

May 28, 2021

94

What Was History?

What was history?

Bunk (Henry Ford)? A pack of tricks played upon the dead (Voltaire)? Hallucinatory impressions of feet in the slime of time (paraphrasing a popular American female poetaster)? My use of the past tense in asking this question is deliberate, not granting credence to the philosophies of Plato and Bishop Berkeley, who believed the essence of reality is derived by the minds of the observers.

Situated as we are, at the ever-unfolding division of a perceived sense of a *now* separating the past from the future, speculation about time lost or regained seems but a clever Proustian literary conceit, useful for understanding "who was who" and "who did what" but without much relevance to our ongoing limited lives. The famous comment by philosopher George Santayana in *The Life of Reason* (1905), "Those who cannot remember the past are condemned to repeat it," is as relevant today as when he wrote it.

Historiography, though, is something else. In a review of two books by Donald Bloxham, *Why History?* and *History and Mortality* (both published by Oxford University Press), in the current *Literary Review*, reviewer Alexandre Leskanich sagely observes that the historicized world is not "just the world 'shaped' by history (by what has previously happened), but also by what is historically known about it." Fact and myth can both be said to be valid in the sense that each makes assertions about events preceding the *now*, whether those events transpired or not.

The proven forgery of the *Protocols of the Elders of Zion* and the account by Gibbon of the *Decline and Fall of the Roman Empire* are both examples of historiography, the former false and the latter true, but both have had consequences for history itself, not only in historiography.

This is why Bloxham makes the point that historians, and all who take an interest in the history of ideas, need to make moral judgments about the writing of history. False assertions, like "fake news," merit being exposed to the fresh air of truth, lest they contribute to further exacerbation of despair, facilitating the inevitable approach of self-induced human extinction.

One who writes about history must necessarily make choices not only about what to include in a narrative but also what is left out, and the choices made will reflect the views of the historian. The magnificent trilogy *Pax Britannica* (1968–1978) by Jan Morris was celebrated as an account of the rise and fall of the British Empire, deemed worthy to occupy the same shelf as Gibbon's *Decline and Fall of the Roman Empire*. But they differ in that Morris was English, writing about her own land, while Gibbon wrote about ancient history, not having to render an impartial account of his own society. But revisionist histories have now been written by those who were subjects of the British Empire, and these authors have their own origins that will colour their decisions about what to include or leave out.

June 4, 2021

95

The Buckmaster Trilogy, Part I: *The Wake*

Author Paul Kingsnorth's first novel in the Buckmaster Trilogy, *The Wake*, is a work of historical fiction set in England over the two years during and following the Norman invasion in 1066. Upon the novel's release in 2014, Kingsnorth attracted a torrent of critical praise, including being long-listed for the Man Booker Prize. The title refers to an awakening of resistance among the native Anglo-Saxon English farmers to the conquering French, some rallying behind a leader known today (but not at the time) as Hereward the Wake, in a rebellion that was rapidly suppressed by the invaders.

The story is told by Buccmaster of Holland, the surviving fictional leader of a group of "green men," rebels whose cause eventually fizzled out. This transition from English to Norman culture was a major turning point, a "hinge of history" for those who dwelt on the land, the end not only of a system of laws and government but of language and culture. The narrator rages, mourning his personal losses of land and family, as he vainly tries with a small group of reluctant co-conspirators to defeat the invaders.

Kingsnorth clearly knows his stuff, providing an exhaustive list of twelve primary and forty-two secondary literary sources, locations of where the actions transpired and references to the epic *Beowulf* and the Bayeux Tapestry. An included explanatory essay describes Kingsnorth's research of the known historical information and how it was used throughout the novel. The reader might find this information dry and scholarly, but the text is anything but, for the entire book is written in a "shadow language," employing words of pre-Norman provenance wherever possible, with spelling and sentence structure attempting to be close to that of Old English. A short glossary of terms and pronunciation rules is provided, but much is left to the reader to infer from the context.

An explanatory note by the author reveals how he came to create a text unlike that of other historical novels that employ the full panoply of expressions in contemporary English, often diminishing the strangeness (to us) of the ancient world. Kingsnorth deliberately reinforces how "their world was different from ours, not only in time, but in values, understanding, mythopoesis. Language seemed the best way to convey this."

Kingsnorth thus evokes an unfamiliar aura of our being embedded in a culture eerily recognizable but still alien to our conventional picture of life in the Middle Ages, with the "old gods" still hovering on the margin as French missionaries promote their version of Christianity. While vexed initially by the unfamiliar language portraying the feelings and actions of Buccmaster and the other green men, with time, the persistent reader subtly becomes more comfortable with this unusual mode of expression, which gradually generates a sense of familiarity with the pre-Norman society that is being eroded by the invaders.

May 10, 2021

96

An Evil World

Over a hundred years ago, Dutch historian of ideas Johan Huizinga, when writing about life in the late European Middle Ages, characterized that time as suffused with a "passionate intensity of life." He claimed that events in the Middle Ages displayed greater contrasts between right and wrong, good and evil, hope and fear, than were experienced at the time Huizinga was writing. First titled in an English translation *The Waning of the Middle Ages* (1924), Huizinga's work later appeared as *The Autumn of the Middle Ages* (published in 1996), a seasonal characterization of this period of

European history before the Renaissance. Now, in 2021, it has once again been published, this time as *Autumntide of the Middle Ages*, which attempts to convey the exact meaning of the Dutch original, *Herfsttij der Middeleeuwen* (1919).

Huizinga's work has been esteemed from its first publication for conveying a profound sense of how life was experienced by a mostly subdued and illiterate population ruled by powerful warlords, permeated by Christian doctrine and embedded in a social order consisting of clerics, nobility and commoners. The immediacy of life, with sickness and death never distant, provoked extremes of joy and despair. Punishment by abuse, torture and execution was public and brutal, eagerly watched by enthralled observers. St. Thomas Aquinas (1225–1274) was said to have wondered whether those in heaven who had been saved from eternal damnation could look down upon the suffering of sinners in hell as they were subjected to the punishments they so richly deserved.

Hatred and vengeance characterized the attitude of rulers towards those opposing and disobeying them. Itinerant preachers denounced what they perceived to be sinful, and harsh reprisal was the rule. In the conclusion of the opening chapter of this masterful account, Huizinga wrote,

> It is an evil world. The fires of hatred and violence burn fiercely. Evil is powerful, the devil covers a darkened earth with his black wings. And soon the end of the world is expected. But mankind does not repent, the church struggles, and the preachers and poets warn and lament in vain.

As the Middle Ages waned at different times across Europe, first in Italy and later in the north, a great rebirth, or renaissance, occurred, in which the stagnation of the Middle Ages, characterized by the acceptance of Christian scripture as the ultimate source of understanding, shattered with the rediscovery of the earlier classical cultures of Rome and Greece and the refamiliarization of ancient philosophy.

Centuries later, the Enlightenment appeared, bringing with it the decline of religion and the celebration of reason, empirical observation and the beginnings of "natural philosophy," so called to distinguish it from theology. Natural philosophy eventually came to be known simply as "science." Like the narrator of Marcel Proust's *In Search of Lost Time*, who looked backwards over his life as a conscious human, we too can look behind ourselves, as a species driven to understand ourselves as conscious beings, to where we came from and forward to where we are going.

But the devil has died along with God, and we find ourselves alone in the universe, as the "fires of hatred and violence" continue burning as fiercely as in the autumn of the Middle Ages. And there is no one to blame apart from ourselves. Asked if I thought today's world resembled the late Middle Ages, I said it seems more of a rerun of the Weimar Republic than some fifteenth-century European duchy; besides, the latter ended with the Renaissance, whereas the former ended in the Third Reich.

May 18, 2021

97

The Age of Endarkenment

Like Gandhi's comment about civilization, one might say that enlightenment is a good idea, but regrettably most humans prefer to live in the dark, convinced, as Plato wrote, that the shadows they see in their caves are the real world. When capitalized, Enlightenment refers to the cultural phenomenon dating back to the late seventeenth and eighteenth centuries in Europe, often called the Age of Reason, as there was a shift away from the theological framing of ideas based on scripture to what we now regard as the scientific account of humanity and nature.

Philosophical justification for the shift away from a theological explanation of the world and humankind came from Scotland's John Locke and Continental thinkers like Voltaire and Immanuel

Kant, leading to an understanding of the physical structure of the world through experiment and to political upheavals like the French and American Revolutions. The writings of Enlightenment thinkers inspired the movement towards studying the natural world as an alternative to scripture, as seen in Freemasonry and in secularist movements in general, fiercely condemned by reactionary authoritarians, as seen in the Inquisition in Rome, in which Galileo was condemned in 1633 for advocating heliocentrism. A cultural feature of the Enlightenment was the development of a sense of inevitable social and political evolutionary progress, mirrored in the optimism voiced by Wordsworth when he wrote, "Bliss it was in that dawn to be alive. But to be young was very heaven."

A cultural shift in attitude like this brings to mind how Plato's allegory of the cave can be extended to reflect the physical changes sustained when moving from darkness into light and the reverse. Sudden increase in enlightenment can provoke an abrupt change in how one interprets the world one sees. As when emerging from a cave into bright sunshine, visual discomfort persists until a new retinal adaptation is sustained. Moving back into the cave, however, compels one to move slowly, as vision gradually becomes accustomed to decreased ambient light.

After the horrors of two world wars in the last century and the founding of the United Nations in a renewed spirit of progress, both economic and moral, there was a gradual clouding of the ideal of social democracy and progress, as described by historian Tony Judt in his book *Ill Fares the Land* (2010). Writing over ten years ago, Judt berated the celebration of greed as a virtue in Western society, augmented since the fall of the Berlin Wall in 1989, signalling the demise of communism and triumph of capitalism.

Today, a decade after Judt's howl of dismay, the picture is ever gloomier. Future prospects appear only harsher, mirroring the final days of the Weimar Republic, as the wealthy enrich themselves and the poor sink ever deeper into misery. We are now observing a darkening. What we thought was progress was instead a chimera, and we now suffer the return of tyrants and the devaluation of science. A dystopic future awaits those returning to the darkness and comfort of their cave. An understanding of the world derived only from social media, and read on electronic devices dependent upon stored energy, will continue to decline as the sources of energy become increasingly unavailable.

We are entering an Age of Endarkenment, and we are doomed.

October 18, 2020; revised August 18, 2021

98

Losing Time

How can one lose that which one never possessed? The young may have that illusion, but with age-ripened awareness, all dissolves into memory as days and nights alternate into a series of images, increasingly fleeting, like uncaptured butterflies. Such were the insomniac dreams of Vladimir Nabokov, flitting away as consciousness returned. The incessantly demanding and recurrent *now* is a distraction from the search for "lost time," for physical demands, commanding the emptying of a full bladder or repositioning one's limbs, interrupt reverie, no matter how comfy the nest one constructs at bedtime.

Marx counsels an unsettling reversal, writing in *The Eighteenth Brumaire of Louis Napoleon* that "the past lies like a nightmare upon the present." Einstein leaves open the concepts of past and future, asserting that the *now* looks Janus-like in both directions. But both thermodynamics and quantum mechanics assert unidirectional one-way movement from past to future, characterized by the universal increasing disorder, or entropy, and radioactive decay, respectively. Is searching for lost time, then, a fool's errand?

In his 1997 book *How Proust Can Change Your Life,* Swiss British philosophical writer Alain de Botton suggests that "a genuine homage to Proust would be to look at *our* world through *his* eyes, not to look at *his* world through *our* eyes." This reversal of perspective suggests a readiness to drop long-winded expositions of meaning contained in the overwhelming deluge of words in the seven-volume novel, allowing literary critics to deconstruct the text as they please. The reader, however, can delight in the imagery of the past illuminating the *now* without getting involved in issues of interest to psychoanalysts, Marxists or historians of ideas.

An operatic cycle of *In Search of Lost Time,* akin to Wagner's *Ring of the Nibelung,* might be fun to envisage. However, the lack of dramatic action would seem to assign such a project more to the subdued mood of Claude Debussy's *Pelléas et Mélisande* than to the sweaty dwarves of Nibelheim and the loud, shrieking female warriors of Walhalla.

Time for a cup of tea and a biscuit …

January 18, 2021

99

Jan Morris: Best Before

Jan Morris lived a full and satisfying authorial life, writing, initially, before her gender transition, about the conquering of Everest (1958); about the British Empire (1974) in the esteemed historical trilogy *Pax Britannica*; about her pioneering transition in the short memoir *Conundrum* (1974); and later about her many travels — exuberantly about Manhattan (1987), wistfully about Trieste (2001) — ever acutely sensitive to the sights, sounds, smells and unique historical ambiences of her many destinations.

Morris retired with her partner, Elizabeth, to her beloved corner of northwest Wales, surrounded by her mementos, keeping minimally active by a regular routine of walking a thousand steps daily in all weathers, until finally waving farewell to her readers late last year and departing from this life on her final voyage on December 20, 2020.

Writing to the end, Morris's penultimate book of observations, *In My Mind's Eye: A Thought Diary* (2018), was a collection of thoughts about her life, past and present, and was followed last year by a sequel, *Thinking Again* (2020), the thirty-second and final published book of her long and productive career, in which she shared pungent short reflections about life in her tenth decade. These brief vignettes are not individually dated and have no common theme beyond presenting an opinion, a memory or a thought arising from her daily subdued existence living in retirement and caring for her dear Elizabeth, now sadly fading away with dementia.

Lamenting the loss of values from her early days, Morris also expressed a sense of regret, fearing the approach of the end of things, of living too long, of becoming resigned to just "let it be," of rereading Tolstoy and her own books, but of having a sensible view of mortality. She yet again commends kindness towards others as the prime virtue one can display over life.

The writers of the promotional blurbs cited on the final book's cover justly praise the elegance and sublime prose of a gentle soul approaching the end of her life. Not mentioned, however, are her written reflections on the disgraced former American president Donald J. Trump: "I've always liked his personal style," she wrote. She called him "a man of true abilities," with "forgivably childlike behaviour." Morris even went so far as to suggest that "a second term would be a good deed in a very naughty world."

It seems, however, that Morris may have had second thoughts about this opinion, along with a hint of insight, asking herself if Elizabeth's Alzheimer's dementia was contagious, and musing that perhaps she was just "past my sell-by date."

As much as I love her writing, I am inclined to agree with this concern, and hope as a writer that I will be advised before my own "best before" date ...

March 18, 2021

TIME PRESENT

100

The Measure of Time

Books and articles keep surfacing that address the measure of time, a subject that has become increasingly, er, timely, owing to our rising sense of living on the cusp of fundamental change, as we *progress* from a highly structured and semi-civilized world of individuals to either some form of hive community, aided by artificial intelligence, or a crash into preliterate barbarism. Or perhaps both, as in Paul Kingsnorth's novel *Alexandria*, which paints an imaginary future world divided between these two alternatives.

We measure time based on the Earth's rotation, with devices like sundials, clocks and watches. The history of these time-measuring efforts was recently reviewed in the *New York Review of Books* (*NYRB*). In his book *About Time,* David Rooney, former curator of timekeeping at the Royal Observatory at Greenwich, outlines both the history of horology (the art of making clocks and watches) and, more generally, the study and measurement of time.

But what is *time?*

Rooney declines to discuss that question, saying he will leave it to be elaborated by scientists and philosophers. Following his lead, the *NYRB* review sidesteps this issue. The question is confronted, however, in the August 31, 2021, issue of the e-zine *Quanta*, in which science writer Natalie Wolchover observes that a physicist might say, like Einstein, that time is what is measured by clocks. And while Einstein's theory of general relativity treats time as a fourth dimension, it does not recognize the directionality of time's arrow. This is unlike quantum mechanics, which does, by relating time to entropy, the direction inherent in increasing disorder, as in radioactive decay.

Research in quantum thermodynamics is based on the recognition of a *clock* as anything that decays or changes irreversibly, like a heated object as it cools, dispersing energy to its surroundings and registering an increase in disorder, or entropy.

Recent experiments at Oxford University suggest that time can only be measured imperfectly. Whether there is a limit involving time, such that its measure can only be imperfect, remains to be seen. Physicist Carlo Rovelli, for one, believes time to be not smooth but quantized, like frames in cinema.

Wolchover lucidly describes the great conundrum of contemporary physics, the inability to reconcile quantum mechanics and general relativity, and invokes the question posed by physicists: "Could it be that time is an illusion and smooth time is an emergent consequence of trying to put events into a smooth order? It is certainly an intriguing possibility that is not easily dismissed."

The debate continues, but hints of progress in understanding the "nature of time" continue to appear. It remains to be seen how far this quest will unfold before collapse of civilization upon this doomed planet draws the curtain over scientific enquiry ...

November 13, 2021

101

The Buckmaster Trilogy, Part II: *Beast*

In Paul Kingsnorth's novel *Beast*, the second in the Buckmaster Trilogy, a contemporary man, married and with an infant daughter, becomes completely fed up with the demands of work, family and society. He resolves to, and does, detach himself from these ties, choosing to live as a solitary hermit in an abandoned and decrepit structure somewhere on a moor.

One day early on in his self-isolation, frustrated by stormy weather, he unwisely attempts to repair his roof, which is about to be blown off by wind. While doing so, he falls, grievously injuring himself. Alone and helpless, he manages (unconvincingly) to splint his leg. Despite gradually improving physically, he is unable to find food or seek help because of his extreme isolation. Over an unspecified period, he gradually recovers his ability to walk and begins to explore his surroundings, finding no other people nearby. Briefly catching sight of a large cat, he sets out to find the creature.

His descent into madness, complete with hallucinations and eventually paranoid delusions, is convincingly described by Kingsnorth. His writing is elegant and the sections of the book, like the protagonist's mental state, are fragmented, without clear beginnings or endings, much like dreams. One Goodreads reviewer writes, "This is a vivid exploration of isolation, courage and the search for truth. Short, shocking and exhilarating, it confirms Paul Kingsnorth as one of our most daring and rewarding contemporary writers."

The novel has received conflicting responses — some love it, others hate it. As a psychiatrist, what I see within the pages is the descent into psychotic depression of an individual who has become a hermit in response to the vicissitudes of life in today's society. This response can be seen in parallel and compared against those of Buccmaster of Holland, the protagonist of Kingsnorth's first Buckmaster novel, *The Wake*, who responds to loss of home and family caused by the 1066 Norman invasion by rebelling against the invaders.

The sole protagonist of the short but intense *Beast*, Edward Buckmaster shares more than the surname of his implied predecessor, for both respond to frustration with the stress of life events in their societies by means of displacement of anger, directed outward by rebellion against the Norman invaders in the first book, and inward by social isolation and towards destruction of the self in the second.

Anger and depression are both responses to sources of frustration common to all of us, whether from war, crime, intolerance, betrayal, injury — the list goes on indefinitely, for the world we live in is never totally acceptable to our desires. Religions and other social activities tend to provide support in these circumstances, unless, of course, one is an isolated hermit.

May 11, 2021

102

Scientific Eschatology and the Rebirth of Apocalyptic Literature

My youngest child, an Anglican priest, dropped by the tower of the halfway house where I am presently confined, presenting me with a doorstopper of a new book that describes itself enticingly within the subtitle as *A New History of Humanity*. Coauthored by archaeologist David Wengrow and the late anthropologist David Graeber, its grandiose title, *The Dawn of Everything*, portends a comprehensive picture that is usually suspect in matters involving the history of ideas.

Some critics have described the work as a "revisionist approach" to the understanding of how we have come to be what we are. Of course, reviewers will surely differ in their opinions as to how successfully the authors have made their case about the nature of *Homo sapiens* throughout the ages, driven home in the vast 526 pages of the book. Not yet having read any of it, I can offer no comments about how cogent and consistent with historical facts their theses and arguments appear to be.

Nevertheless, without reading the text one can still ask, why did the authors write this book, at this time? Is it of any value to speculate on the sorry history of our species? It is now abundantly evident that human life on this poisoned planet will no longer be sustainable in the foreseeable future. As humans ignore the science and continue to induce ever more global warming by burning forests and fossil fuels, can anyone expect anything ahead but collapse?

After all, we have passed the point of no return. The end stage will be the death of all humans, accompanying the extinctions of aquatic and terrestrial life induced by human activity. Do we have eyes that cannot see, or ears that cannot hear?

One can speculate about ultimate cause(s) of the coming catastrophe, causes beyond the mere cupidity of human endeavours, of being always greedy for more, fostered by capitalist exploitation of the environment. This Schopenhauerian *will* to power, damn the consequences, suggests a basic drive inherent in living organisms, including humans, that leads them to their own destruction.

In these end times, their certainty endorsed by scientific eschatology, we are sure to witness a rebirth of apocalyptic literature, such as the dystopic novels of authors like Paul Kingsnorth and Michael Christie. But a book about history, one that proclaims to explain "the dawn of everything," is only looking backwards, ignoring the approaching dusk, as Hegel's owl of Minerva is again preparing to spread her grim wings, this time over the final days of humanity.

January 22, 2022

103

The Owl of Minerva

In Greek mythology, a little owl traditionally represented or accompanied Athena, the virgin goddess of wisdom; Minerva was her syncretic incarnation in Roman mythology. Because of such association, the bird — often referred to as the owl of Athena or the owl of Minerva — has been used as a symbol of knowledge, wisdom, perspicacity and erudition throughout the Western world.

The nineteenth-century German idealist G.W.F. Hegel famously wrote in 1820, "the owl of Minerva spreads its wings only with the falling of the dusk," implying that philosophers only come to understand a historical condition as it passes away — in hindsight. Hegel's biographer Klaus Vieweg described this statement as "one of the most beautiful metaphors of the history of philosophy." The image evoked, of the owl preparing to depart, suggests some impending loss of understanding that is not recognized as such until it is too late.

This metaphor is perhaps more accessible to the student of the history of ideas than the usual metaphysical verbiage emanating from the dense Teutonic forests of philosophical idealism, and one can appropriate it for use in other contexts, such as describing Tony Judt's book *Postwar* (2005), which clarifies the consequences of the Second World War a half century after its conclusion, or in many contemporary retrospective accounts of the British Empire written by those from its former possessions.

The lessons of history, however relevant to contemporary issues, are quickly forgotten, as observed by Santayana and mocked by Marx, for although the owl of Minerva may pay us a call, she does not linger, and we are condemned to repeat our errors as farce, tragedy, or perhaps both, like Napoleon's retreat from Moscow in 1812 or the American fiascos in Southeast Asia in the twentieth century and Afghanistan in the twenty-first.

Historical time can be thought of in terms of either events that initiate a dramatic change, such as a revolution or an assassination, or of durations, like an ongoing period distinct from that which preceded it. Martin Luther's famous direct challenge to Rome was an event, the Reformation that followed, a new historical period of time. Invoking history implies time in the sense of a moment, not as duration. The owl's visit may represent an event, a sudden and unanticipated realization, perhaps an epiphany leading to some significant shift in direction. On a more individual and psychological level, a psychedelic experience may be thought of this way if it facilitates some profound change in one's life, like a change in career or religious belief.

For me, the owl of Minerva has been a reminder of what I still recall from age four, when I was taught to read by an aunt: that a successful life depends on education, and that learning is a worthwhile, lifelong activity. Later, when I learned of Hegel's connecting the idea of historical understanding with the owl of Minerva spreading her wings at dusk, the bird became endowed with a powerful message of persisting with the tasks of learning before it's too late.

Upon visiting my room in the tower in which I now reside, guests are greeted by a replica of an owl by Picasso, as well as five miniature owls adorning the bookcases, with their collective burden of information, all acquired before digitization and not requiring a connection to the internet. My books will still be there in the event of a power failure. Works of science, history, music, travel and language on the east wall; biography, literature, drama and art on the west. All guarded by replicas of the owl of Minerva perched above them.

Although I live alone, these books are my friends and companions; they constitute my wealth of words and embody my portfolio of ideas.

October 8, 2021

104

Halfway House

The term *halfway house* is commonly used to describe temporary intermediate accommodations for those unhappy souls who have either just been paroled from prison or who have fully withdrawn and completed their program at a substance-addiction treatment facility. Supportive residential programs like halfway houses have demonstrated that these temporary group homes lower the rate of recidivism among parolees or of relapse among substance abusers, providing them a sheltered and secure space to live alongside support with only minimal restrictions, allowing for a gradual return to "normal" independent functioning.

Movement through this kind of system may also be considered bidirectional, such as for those moving in the reverse direction, from initial independent living to a semi-supportive ("halfway") facility, in which services like meals, recreational activities and minimal care are provided for the inmates (tactfully called *residents*) until they relocate to their final establishments, i.e., chronic care homes or the morgue. Residents living in these places are encouraged to continue with as many of their usual activities and pastimes as possible, and to bring along with them familiar items from their previous homes with which to decorate their new surroundings, in an effort to minimize the transition as much as possible, given the limitations imposed by age or disability.

These facilities often display subtle names like Sunset Lodge or Resthaven, reflecting their purpose as an end-of-life accommodation. Their architecture reflects the needs of the resident population, with extra-wide doorways and hallways that provide enhanced access to those with personal mobility devices and stout handrails along each corridor wall for those who continue afoot, often with a cane or stick because of balance difficulties, to prevent them from falling.

Accommodation provided may vary from a studio to a one-bedroom suite, depending on the facility and resident preference, and facilities may provide furniture or allow residents to bring their own. Compact washrooms often contain showers with ledges for those who prefer to shower seated (again, to avoid falls). Meal services are overseen by a nutritionist familiar with the needs of an elderly population: with intake balanced among food groups, minimally salted, appropriately portioned as "senior sized" (i.e., small) and with attention paid to special needs of diabetics and those with food allergies or intolerances. Residents may be asked to wear a signalling device that can be used to alert staff of need for help, as in the case of a fall, injury or other medical emergency. Staff would then assess the need for first aid or further medical attention, which would then be summoned.

Social interactions are encouraged among those residing in these "halfway homes," to promote a sense of community and to prevent isolation and possible solitary morbid thinking. In addition to other forms of divertissement, like television, games and cinema, sexual expression between residents is possible within the privacy of their suites. The elderly have sexual needs as do younger people, and having the opportunity to satisfy them appropriately is important to their mental health. In a talk to a group of queer men about aging, American psychiatrist Loren Olson described one residence he knew that boasted of two retired gay gentlemen who met every Friday morning before lunch in each other's rooms to give one another blow jobs.

Clearly, these "halfway houses" for the elderly fulfill a need among many who survive into significant old age "thanks to the miracles of modern medicine." Unfortunately, this option is not available to most, for access is limited to those in our Western culture who can afford to pay for it. And for those who can't, care is usually left to available family members to manage as best as they can. In the absence of any willing or able support in this situation, many of those who would benefit from this type of semi-independent living situation end up alone, a known risk to falls and premature mortality.

October 4, 2021

105

Death Row and Segregation

One month after leaving my cozy neighbourhood apartment, where I had been living happily for ten years, and relocating to a barely affordable but pleasant "retirement community" in an industrial/commercial zone, featuring independent suites and minimal services like meals and cleaning, I reflected on my abrupt shift to a very different physical and social environment. At first impression, it seemed to me that one could compare "retirement communities" with penal colonies (like Kafka's) and "halfway houses," each having its own criteria for segregating its members from the general population: age for the former, crime and substance abuse for the latter.

Unlike in most "civilized" countries, within some prisons in the US (notoriously so) is an area known as "death row," which further segregates those inmates sentenced to be executed by the state from other prisoners. On the other hand, in "retirement communities," *all* residents could be thought of as being at least in the preliminary stage of death row, their "crimes" being that of having lived too long, likely with some measure of physical disability. Living here at the "halfway house" full time, surrounded by fellow inmates (most with mobility problems) and the younger, nearly all female staff, reinforces the stark fact of voluntarily having entered an age-segregated area.

"Stone walls do not a prison make, nor iron bars a cage," wrote poet Richard Lovelace in 1649. True, yet at times I feel like a condemned prisoner, always alone in my comfortable "cell," awaiting death, my crimes being not only age but also my education, that fatal combination resulting in the curse of Cassandrism, an awareness of an impending negative event that others ignore or deny, exacerbated by social isolation.

The retirement "community" provides distraction, with organized fun and games, cinema, excursions, lectures and so on, but age segregation is only further emphasized by these group activities. All men and women are mortal, and of course we are all on death row, but the constant reminder of it by the institutional milieu and by being surrounded almost exclusively by fellow inmates is bitter.

But ruminating on one's life situation is not only non-productive but depressogenic. Being a writer (among other things), I deal with the situation by writing about it. After all, the only solution to old age is early death.

C'est la vie.

November 1, 2021

106

Misanthropy and Benevolence

Although often associated with older curmudgeons like myself, misanthropy — a strong dislike (at times rising to frank hatred) of other human beings — may be expressed by individuals of any age.

A friend who volunteered to work for a Canadian international aid agency (CUSO) in West Africa for three years said upon his return that having been a cynic before he left, he had now become a misanthrope. His typical misanthropic reaction to the current war in Eastern Europe was summarized in a one-word sneer: humans!

Living to an advanced, or "ripe," old age is the result of "miracles of modern medicine," repeatedly deferring death with surgical interventions like joint replacements, pacemakers, shunts, stents and grafts, as well as with prescription medical pharmaceutical agents. Little can be done, though, about cognitive failure, such as Alzheimer's, and other neurological conditions, like ALS.

Bodies eventually wear out or succumb to untreatable neoplastic diseases (cancer) and other chronic conditions. Media prognostications of extending life on and on usually ignore the realities of time and gravity doing their work on once healthy and limber bodies. Appearing youthful is big business, not only for the cosmetics industry but also for purveyors of hearing aids, spectacles, dentures, wigs, etc., and mobility devices from sticks and canes to propelled wheelchairs. Residences for the elderly advertise amenities like commodious suites, gourmet meals and organized activities, with advertisements showing the beaming, youthful faces of satisfied residents enjoying their retirement. No doubt some do, and some don't. Among the latter are the geriatric misanthropes, grumbling about how miserable their lives have become.

It is still possible to enjoy life while dwelling in an aging body. One can even feel misanthropic about humanity at large yet at the same time retain a sense of benevolence towards others. Such is the case of my old Africa pal, now enjoying his declining years making model airplanes and being a loving grandfather, cultivating his garden, taking life as it comes in the present. After all, the only way to avoid the vicissitudes of old age is to die young.

March 3, 2022

107

Cremains

A portmanteau word, *cremains* signifies "cremated remains," with the latter full expression being preferred by those in the trade of disposing of corpses by vapourizing them in specially designed furnaces called crematoria. While until recently burial in a casket "six feet under" has traditionally been the practice in Christian societies that promise an "afterlife," cremation has long been used in other cultures. Historically, there is evidence of the practice dating back 17,000 years, documented in records and findings from prehistoric Australia.

In the process of cremation, all liquids and non-metallic solids are converted to vapour, leaving behind only bone, which is subsequently ground into powder and returned to the family for disposal or storage in an urn. It may also be kept *in memoriam* at a niche in a columbarium designed for that purpose. Commonly called *ashes*, these cremains are not literally ashes but rather the ground bone meal not vapourized in the furnace.

Prior to cremation, implanted medical devices are removed from the corpse, for pacemakers may explode in the heat of the furnace and orthopedic bone replacements made of titanium cannot be vapourized, and are generally later sold by the crematorium as scrap metal.

Commercial enterprises vie with one another to sell a full range of cremation services, from the cheap no-nonsense approach to the elaborate "full-service" models, wherein additional extras can be purchased as add-ons, such as memorial services and special urns for the cremains. Prepaid disposal is readily available from many local memorial societies, removing the need to decide from mourning friends and family, who are more concerned with loss and memories of the deceased than with the niceties of disposal or organic remains.

Concerns may remain, however, regarding the disposal of the cremains. This may reflect different views among family members of what to do with them or differing options about location of the burial site, perhaps due to inconsistent choices of the deceased as expressed at different times of their lives. Often, religious values of the family and community expectations play a clear role in the decision making.

The final decision of location, however, is necessarily the choice of the recipient of the cremains, not the wish of the deceased, for once gone, the dearly departed have no opinion regarding the site of their final resting place. Whatever location is decided upon reflects the wish of the one who inters, not the interred.

July 17, 2020

108

Obituaries

While an epitaph on a gravestone or tomb is generally celebratory about the life of the deceased, and is expected to endure the passage of time, an obituary, contrastingly, is but an immediate announcement of a "passing away" for those who may be interested in receiving that information.

A recent essay in the *Times Literary Supplement* by D.J. Taylor, about how to go about writing an obituary, caught my eye, not because I either intend to write one or expect one to be written about me after my departure (for whatever circle to which I'll be assigned in the Inferno), but simply because I enjoy writing about people and ideas.

According to Taylor, in not wishing to speak ill of the dead, obituaries tend to display a certain measure of obfuscation, in that the writer avoids any direct reference to characteristics or tendencies of the deceased that may appear negative or unappealing to a reader. Thus, a heavy drinker may be described as a "connoisseur of malt beverages," or, when referring to the subject's gay eroticism in the days before it became generally accepted as but a facet of one's personality, with the coy circumlocution (one of my favourites) "one of those unlucky men in whom the passions are misdirected."

Opinions of the obituary writer are often assumed to be neutral, but when the deceased is known personally, the writer's opinion may off-handedly sneak its way into the text, suggesting a hint of admired positive traits or values. When the subject is generally disliked, such as powerful figures known for their wickedness, like Hitler or Stalin, avoiding suggestion of the unpleasant odour of putrefaction may be difficult.

Taylor also recounts many entertaining examples of obituaries, both from fiction and from the past lives of the famous, illustrating the tricky business of describing the dead. Some current obituarist's code phrases include "enjoyed a variegated social life" ("light-minded boulevardier"); "flamboyant" ("irksome scene-stealer"); and "larger than life" ("tedious show-off"). "No respecter of reputations," often used to describe literary or dramatic critics, tends to mean simply "rude," as does "teasing sense of humour."

Evidently, Taylor enjoys the delicious prose of obituaries composed by fellow writers. Much of the fun derives from hinting about the quirks and foibles of the subject, removing the writer from the threat of legal action from his victim while alive. That ubiquitous useful source of information that is Wikipedia issues a stern warning to those hastily composing descriptions of celebrities before their passing: "Contentious material about living persons that is unsourced or poorly sourced must be removed immediately, especially if potentially libelous or harmful." As an alternative, excessive praise may be seen as ironic. It may be tempting to imagine Taylor's own obituary, but probably inadvisable to publish it.

One of the advantages of not being well known is that one is not likely to be the subject of an obituary, for few will care one way or the other whether one lives or dies.

July 8, 2021

109

Last Words and Epitaphs

Although I usually think of Beethoven raising his fist and scowling instead of verbalizing any profound last words, the concept of final utterances is familiar to all of us, and an internet search for famous last words yields a variety of wit, wisdom and well-wishes. Ever the esthete, Oscar Wilde (1854–1900), in his cheap Parisian hotel room, said, "Either that wallpaper goes or I do." Unable to summon up any wit like Wilde, Winston Churchill (1874–1965) observed, "I'm bored with it all."

Another set of last words I remember well is found in one of the six volumes of the "autobiographical novel" *My Struggle,* by Norwegian author Karl Ove Knausgård. Knausgård tells the story of a national television celebrity who, when asked what his last words might be, responded, "When taking a shower standing in the bathtub, one should *never* forget to make sure the shower curtain lies *inside* the rim of the bathtub, otherwise you get water all over the floor."

Unlike last words, epitaphs, tend to be more serious, engraved upon tombstones, plaques and monuments, a short text honouring the deceased. For example, the tombstone of philosopher Immanuel Kant in Königsberg is inscribed with his words "The Moral Law in us, and the starry Heaven above us." A fitting epitaph for the "father of the Enlightenment." The emperor Augustus composed his own, a vainglorious paean to his wisdom and political and military accomplishments. There are hundreds of blue plaques affixed to buildings in and around London that are epitaphs calling attention to famous writers and others, of interest no doubt to the curious passersby who may have heard of them previously, but like all such inscriptions they are ephemeral and will succumb to the ravages of time, as will we all.

Changing social values lead to re-evaluation of individuals formerly esteemed. This may lead to political iconoclasm, the destruction of images or statues of those once admired but who have fallen out of favour because of having owned slaves or engaged in some other activity now deemed reprehensible, such as imperial conquest. Newspapers and other media sites thrive on the photogenicity of the beheading of statues or of casting them into the sea, but iconoclasm is an old tradition. Annual Guy Fawkes bonfires in the UK every November 5 celebrate the failure of the 1605 gunpowder plot, and immolation of a straw effigy confers some measure of vicarious satisfaction to onlookers.

If I were asked what my last words might be, in the spirit of Knausgård I might reply that before my useless corpse is flung into the fiery furnace of the crematorium, the stoker must first remove the pacemaker, otherwise it will explode in the intense heat and make a mess in the oven.

August 7, 2021; revised December 28, 2021

110

On Reaping Whirlwinds

Hosea, the first of the twelve minor prophets in the Jewish bible, wrote in the seventh verse of Chapter 8, "For they sow the wind, and they shall reap the whirlwind." Leave it to an ancient Hebrew prophet to come up with a succinct statement about climate.

As tornados rage over the American Bible Belt, the inclement and destructive weather, associated with the phenomenon of global warming, itself the consequence of the industrial revolution and the subsequent capitalist iniquities and abominations promoting consumerism and fostered by advertising, is now leading to the extinction of humanity by making the planet uninhabitable. But we should consider other afflictions as well, like pestilence, as we socially isolate during this first viral pandemic of the twenty-first century. I say *first* because there will certainly be others, facilitated by crowded cities and the intercontinental movement of human vectors, together spreading lethal infections by air travel to all six continents.

Inane youths, sharing recirculated air, flying from Canada to Mexico, wildly partying while confined in an airplane, doubtless ensured that the current pestilence that is COVID-19 is shared among as many victims as possible. And COVID is only a "natural" pestilence. There may be more coming of a non-natural provenance, for weaponization of scientific advances has been well documented throughout human history. In olden times catapults flung rats over the walls of besieged cities to induce plague. Today we have viral labs instead of catapults, awaiting orders to proceed with intentionally sowing their whirlwinds of fabricated virions among perceived enemies.

Another traditional divine punishment is famine, especially for those who worship a wrong god like mammon (wealth regarded as an object of worship and devotion), the pursuit of which is sanctified by capitalism in the neoliberal economic system under which humankind is now congealed.

And then there is the loss of arable land caused by the destruction of rainforests, and desertification attributed to climate change, guaranteeing the coming scarcity of food. This will be felt initially among the poor, but later come to affect the wealthy nations all the same, those now flying in out-of-season foodstuffs from the opposite hemisphere to grace the tables of their citizens, while the cargo aircraft used in their transportation increases global warming. This is more than an iniquity, it is an abomination to Gaia.

But Mother Earth will have her revenge. As famine becomes widespread, wars will inevitably erupt from conflict over *Lebensraum*. Unlike old Hosea, this essay is not a call to repent; it's too late for that now. It is only meant to be a statement of what is what. We will all reap the whirlwinds sowed by the industrial revolution.

January 8, 2022

111

Frustration, Anger, Violence

Antipode is an influential academic journal in the discipline of geography. Relevant to the impending catastrophic collapse of civilization as the result of global warming, the journal recently printed a review of the book *White Skin, Black Fuel* by Andreas Malm and the Zetkin Collective, which examines the relationship between climate denial and resurgent fascism, with white supremacy exhibited by extremist right-wing political parties around the world.

Values similar to those expounded by the far right in many nations may also be observed within the fossil fuel industry, such that defence of the former becomes inseparable from the latter. This situation is obvious nowhere more so than in North America, where the Republican party in the US and the Conservatives in Canada both promote legislation protective of the fossil fuel industry, criminalizing mainly Indigenous-led protests against its infrastructure, some successful enough to constitute a real threat. Malm and the Zetkin Collective conclude that the climate catastrophe cannot be mitigated without confronting fascism.

Malm's 2021 book *How to Blow Up a Pipeline: Learning to Fight in a World on Fire* promotes the view that sabotage of devices that produce CO_2 is a reasonable means of climate activism, for it discourages investment in them in the first place. He is critical of pacifism within the climate movement, referencing the psychiatrist Frantz Fanon, who wrote of liberation movements combating colonialism in the twentieth century, asserting that violence "frees the native from despair and inaction, making him fearless and restoring self-respect."

A contemporary instance of sabotage in the context of climate change was evident this winter (2022) in northern British Columbia, where a group of about twenty unknown violent protestors with axes raided a remote work camp of the Coastal GasLink pipeline, smashing vehicles, using heavy machinery to first destroy buildings and other infrastructure before incapacitating the equipment altogether. The company estimated the cost of the damage amounted to millions of dollars. (There were no injuries among the workers based at the camp, who were driven to safety by security guards.)

Attacks like these, of what has been called "ecological Leninism," are unsurprising, being harbingers of what we can expect to see throughout the coming years, as the frustration and anger of individuals boil over into violent action, while our governments continue to protect and promote the fossil fuel industry.

February 24, 2022

112

Realism, Not Optimism

In a recent essay contributed to *The Conversation (Canada)*, two UBC professors do a wonderful job of considering an appropriate response to the climate crisis affecting humanity. In their essay, titled "The Climate Crisis Demands Courage Not Optimism," political scientist Kathryn Harrison and climate scientist Simon Donner acknowledge the current situation and suggest courage as the only alternative to abandoning hope, in turn leading to denial, drugs, distraction or suicide. Harrison and Donner concede, "As climate researchers, we're keenly aware that it's going to get worse. There is no 'new normal.'"

The Intergovernmental Panel on Climate Change has reported that it is "unequivocal" that *Homo sapiens* is the cause. The results are obviously dire, and news media regularly report the worldwide scale of destruction, by floods, heat domes, wildfires and atmospheric pollution, besetting human beings on every continent.

The industrial revolution's turn to the extraction and burning of fossil fuels is undeniably a primary source of global warming, and the political dedication to the myth of human "progress," coupled with capitalist economic systems that encourage greed, continue even now to drive increased atmospheric warming.

While there are actions that could be done to retard the rate of heating, it seems unlikely that the powers that be have the will to globally collaborate in minimizing it. Harrison and Donner quote Kate Marvel, associate research scientist at NASA, who wonders whether we have the "courage to act." All 7.9 billion of us?

That remains to be seen, but our inborn drives to personally succeed suggest against the possibility of combined action. Schopenhauerian *will*, manifesting in all nature, includes all us greed-driven humans, trumping logical decisions to do what would be necessary only to *retard* the rate. It will now never be reversed. According to the *Guardian,* "Demand for oil and gas has rebounded strongly as the global economy bounces back from the economic slowdown triggered by the COVID-19 pandemic in 2020, leading to a global gas supply crunch and rocketing energy market prices."

Anger and rage are increasing. Reports of northward migration by Canadian border officials are harbingers of what is to come, as climate refugees stream away from areas becoming uninhabitable. A parlous future awaits those of us now living and the yet unborn, for we have passed the point of no return.

January 26, 2022

113

Normal's Overrated

Genesis of a train of thought: when aroused from a reverie, ensconced in my comfy chair after a glass of milk and a peanut butter and jelly sandwich given to me by a volunteer caller from Pacific Opera Victoria, my muse suggested I write a new blog post/essay on something, perhaps starting with the phrase "It is not inevitable that _____ ..."

She instructed me to "fill in the blank!" to get started. How about, "It is not inevitable that one has to be normal ..."?

I have a T-shirt that proclaims, NORMAL'S OVERRATED, a slogan from a TV series years ago called *House*. I never saw the show, but I liked the sentiment, and once wore the shirt at a Pride festival on a hot summer Sunday afternoon in the gay aughties, here in sedate Victoria, BC, where another attendee spontaneously commented that he admired it (presumably meaning the motto on the T-shirt, not its contents).

So, I began to type:

It is not inevitable that daily life here and elsewhere will "return to normal," as regularly intoned by the media, as well as overheard in general conversation while waiting for the bus or in a queue for a jab of vaccine. Yes, the pandemic is subsiding. Though periodic and repeated flare-ups in hot spots, driven by naturally occurring viral variants, continue to be sustained by a reservoir of anti-vaxxers, who curiously disguise their fear, ignorance or both by a veneer of asserting their "love of freedom."

Poisoned by uncritical addiction to exploitative social media platforms that are designed to produce information about likes and dislikes that can be useful in designing merchandise whose sale will enhance profit for the manufacturers and corporate shareholders, social media may circulate false information about vaccination. Whatever happened to the veneration of public health, so hard-won in the nineteenth century by scientific epidemiologists like Marcel's father, Doctor Adrien Proust, whose goal was the extension and preservation of good health?

Global life expectancy has more than doubled in a century. This is why in developed countries like Canada, we now have senior residences, like where I reside with other aged citizens, each of us awaiting our inevitable end, seeking distraction by playing card games, watching TV or writing essays.

If this is the new normal, it's overrated.

December 4, 2021

114

The Shape of Things to Come

In September 1933, the English author H.G. Wells published a science fiction novel titled *The Shape of Things to Come,* imagining what he believed to be the future prospects of humanity. Some of what he projected indeed transpired before long, like social instability, wars, the destruction of population centres by aerial bombardment and weapons of mass destruction. What Wells predicted in the long term, however, erroneously foresaw a utopian state of beneficent world government.

This and other books of Wells's, along with other science-fiction authors like Isaac Asimov, Robert Heinlein and Poul Anderson, were influential in subsequent imaginings of the future. Missing from these early accounts of science fiction, however, were what has now become the major determinant of the future of humanity: the phenomenon of global warming. Today, irreversible atmospheric poisoning and oceanic warming are steadily transforming the climate into one incompatible with human survival, indicating a limited future for *Homo sapiens* upon the surface of this planet.

Enraged crowds of uneducated deniers of science and reason are already making themselves known in "civilized" regions of the world like the US and Canada, promoted by jingoist appeals to "freedom" and incited by capitalist billionaires. No doubt, they may be expected to arise elsewhere, as pseudo-democratic states become replaced by dictatorships, ostensibly to provide order and stability. They too, however, will eventually become unstable, unable to maintain calm in the face of increasing pressure among their citizens. Thermodynamically, this social and political cycle resembles increasingly agitated molecules in a sealed container when subjected to continually increasing external heat, or more biologically, like a live frog in water, whose temperature is cruelly being raised to boiling.

When it comes to understanding reasons for this unhappy state of affairs, it is not necessary to look beyond the common behaviour of all species to modify their environment to ensure procreative success through niche construction. This basic principle of life itself leads to the "balance of nature," in which predators and prey both manage to survive. The predators don't eat every one of the prey, of which enough survive to reproduce, ensuring the continuation of both species.

This balance now has been overcome by the ability of humans to survive without predators, now able to uncontrollably reproduce, defer death and practise extensive niche modification, like the burning of fossil fuels and razing of forests, to an extent destructive of the environment. This is not unlike that of a successful virus replicating itself out of existence by killing its host. Such is the real, not imaginary, shape of things to come.

Vale humanitate.

February 21, 2022

115

The Hinge of Time

What we call the *now* is the subjective impression of a *hinge* of time, upon which swings the division between conscious memory and anticipation. It is the eternal Janus position dividing the past from the future, not a fixed point but a constantly shifting direction of attention, of looking behind or ahead.

For most of us, if we think at all about the concept of time, it is as a moment or a duration, a flow — "time's arrow" pointing only in one direction. For a physical scientist, however, it is also a dimension, and while general relativity theory cannot account for the directionality of time's arrow, quantum thermodynamics can. Entropy is a one-way phenomenon, wherein increasing disorder in a closed system eventually results in equilibrium or stasis. For example, the "heat death" of the universe will result when all energy has been converted into thermal radiation, with none left to perform work.

But as Julian Barbour points out in his book *The Janus Point,* the universe is not a closed system. On the contrary, we can observe the universe expanding from a presumed initial singularity into a sea of quarks that condensed into particles and then hydrogen atoms, and from there became galaxies, stars and assorted leftovers, like what we call the Earth. This is *increasing* complexity, negative entropy — entaxy.

What we call living matter, or life, exhibits the same process of increasing complexity. Utilizing radiation energy from a nearby star to survive and replicate through Darwinian natural selection, over time complex organisms developed a brain, and in humans, eventually conscious self-awareness — a tiny bit of organic matter in the universe seeking to understand itself. In this way, the history of the universe becomes one of self-knowledge.

What this portends for the future of humanity can only be extrapolated from the past, and the historical record is not encouraging. Yet as I suspect, even if humanity succeeds in destroying itself along with the planet, the phenomenon of life has likely arisen elsewhere. We cannot assume that the appearance of humanity as sentient beings thinking about their origin, existence and future has been, is or will ever be unique throughout the universe.

November 18, 2021

TIME FUTURE

116

The Buckmaster Trilogy, Part III: *Alexandria*

This third and final book of Paul Kingsnorth's The Buckmaster Trilogy appeared in late 2020 to mixed critical response. In contrast to *The Wake* and *Beast*, *Alexandria* is a work of dystopic science fiction, set 900 years in the future, involving basic questions of the individual, society, artificial intelligence and the "soul of Mother Earth." Ostensibly, it is a tale of the few surviving members of a religious cult, dying out in a corner of an earth that is gradually reclaiming itself following an ecological apocalypse.

In Kingsnorth's fictional future, most human beings have entirely abandoned their physical bodies, willingly attaining immortality as participants in a posthuman "hive-mentality" known as Alexandria, presumably named for the ancient Egyptian repository of the sum of all knowledge, the Wikipedia of classical antiquity.

In the course of a quest to attain enlightenment, the cult members are besieged by agents of Alexandria and its founder, Wayland (the name appears to reference the Norse mythological figure Wayland the Smith, forger of metal). These Alexandria agents, called "stalkers," are shapeshifting entities (Are they angels? Demons?) whose purpose is to entice, presumably with force if necessary, the few surviving humans to voluntarily abandon their mortal bodies, escape the curse of humanity and ascend into Alexandria.

This convoluted tale is primarily couched in a denatured English, with attention given to peculiar spelling and grammar. Yet when a stalker seeks to convince an immature young male cult adherent to abandon his body, the novel's language abruptly becomes that of the present day, as the protagonist, embodying its author, begins to lecture, describing dire predictions of, namely, the impending doom generated by our human activity, views already well known from Kingsnorth's earlier non-fiction writing in *Uncivilization* (2009) and *Confessions of a Recovering Environmentalist* (2017).

While Kingsnorth's ideas of impending apocalypse are plausible and merit wide dissemination, their explicit fictional presentation in *Alexandria* seems jarring and pedantic. Even Tolstoy refrained from explicitly incorporating his views about history into the text of *War and Peace*, deferring their exposition into separate essays. After the remarkable shadow language of *The Wake* and the psychological sophistication of *Beast*, *Alexandria* seems disappointingly contrived. Kingsnorth can do better; his message is worth it.

May 14, 2021

117

The Buckmaster Trilogy

Taken together, the three books of Kingsnorth's Buckmaster Trilogy can be thought of as a fictional representation of the world as it is constituted, the relationship of humans to their environment and an imagined possible response to the overwhelming and mutually shared destructive hatred so characteristic of our species. It is only a matter of informing oneself from available news sources to observe how blame is routinely assigned to individuals because of their skin colour, religious belief, political adherence, economic status, intelligence, etc. This blaming leads to mutual hatreds and persecutions, and while those that preach harmony among us are commendable, they are overall ineffective.

In the 1980s, songwriter and mathematician Tom Lehrer cynically mocked these well-intentioned but often hypocritical attempts to foster universal acceptance in his lyrics about the once-promoted Brotherhood Week in the US. Available on the internet for all to read, and to subsequently shake their heads at, Lehrer's lyrics echo the aphorisms about public moral hypocrisy by the earlier witty, sage journalist H.L. Mencken in the 1930s.

Underlying rejection of those unlike oneself seems to be a universal characteristic of living matter (though symbiosis may occur between different species when advantageous to both). This is reflected in humans with the competitive drive to excel, not only in sports and games (Faster! Higher! Stronger!) but in the motivators to greed and accumulation, manifestations of what we see in all kinds of life, ranging from viral replication to vegetation seeking sunlight and animal species employing predation to survive and reproduce, including human animals.

Life itself, then, is what drives competition among us, leading to blame and hatred. Nineteenth-century thinkers asked, What is to be done? Schopenhauer argued that it is futile to resist the pressure of the inexorable *will* characteristic of all living organisms. This is the fundamental substrate of Kingsnorth's trilogy. The first book, *The Wake*, illustrates the futility of rebellion and armed force in the maintenance of group survival. In the second, *Beast*, an individual's withdrawal from society is seen to be counterproductive. The concluding volume, *Alexandria*, presents one possible way around the conundrum: the elimination of corporeal, living humans and the inclusion of only their minds in an organized system not dependent upon survival by growth and reproduction. But that sounds not only unlikely but impossible.

Kingsnorth's conclusion, then, is that there is no solution, and that all an individual can do is to understand the human condition, not to change it, for it is a necessary consequence of living matter to be ultimately constrained by entropy. So be kind to others if you can and ameliorate the unhappy but inescapable consequences of being alive.

May 16, 2021

118

Back to Normal?

Asked in the early spring of 2020 by my masked congenial lawyer, following the biennial review of my will, "So when do you think things will get back to normal?" He shook his head with surprise when I told him that in my opinion, things would *never* get back to what was once considered "normal."

Dr. Friederike Otto from the University of Oxford, one of the many authors on the report from the UN's Intergovernmental Panel on Climate Change (IPCC), stated, "Climate change is not a problem of the future, it's here, and now affecting every region in the world." The real strength of the IPCC's new report is the confidence of the assertions that the scientists are now making. The phrase "very likely" appears forty-two times within the forty-odd pages of the "Summary for Policymakers." In scientific terms, that's about 90 to 100 percent certainty of something being real.

The clearest of the report's points is about the responsibility of humanity for climate change. There's no longer any equivocating — it's us, and it's no surprise. Human responsibility for environmental degradation was evident to me while in university seventy years ago, and it has only continued to be endorsed by the scientific community, alongside the continual release of corroborating factual information, from as early as when the Gaia hypothesis, which stated that the embedded life forms on our planet interact with their surrounding inorganic environment to form a co-dependent and self-regulating system, and from which the climate and biochemical conditions allowing life on Earth to exist was developed, was put forward by the chemist James Lovelock and microbiologist Lynn Margulis in the 1970s.

Apart from science, many post-Enlightenment thinkers were also aware of the human propensity for self-destruction. Schopenhauer, Hobbes, Kant, Freud and Berlin all wrote about this, as did authors of fiction, ranging from Kafka, whose Gregor Samsa awakens transformed from uneasy dreams into a loathsome insect in the novella *The Metamorphosis*, to contemporary Canadian novelist Michael Christie, with his concept of the "withering" of trees in the dystopic near future in his 2019 novel *Greenwood*.

But the world at large continues in spite of clear warnings, for as is foolishly said, hope springs eternal. Yet billions will surely perish in the unfolding horrors of the twenty-first century, with normally sedate citizens transforming into crazed fighters for whatever scarce necessities of life remain, like pure water and food.

Bunkers with water, food and weapons will not save you, my lawyer friends. You will suffer and die like the rest of us, for we have passed the point of no return. Our electric cars and efficient air conditioners will only add to the rate of global warming and desertification, for the manufacture and use of appliances and vehicles all lead to dissipation of heat in the making and using of them.

End times are upon us, and supernatural ideation will no doubt flourish as science is foolishly abandoned by anti-vaxxers and other deniers shutting their eyes to what is obvious, closing their minds to reason and well-established scientific fact, and thereby hastening the impending collapse of civilization. Uncontrolled viral pandemics will be the new normal.

August 9, 2021

119

Beyond Misanthropy

The pagan image of the wheel of Ixion is that of life turning relentlessly, undeterred by either hope or the rage and despair of all who deny hope, progressing continually towards a stable existence. We seem compelled by our human nature to confront the self-destructive consequences of our own ignorance.

Social collapse, or the disappearance of long-held group norms and expectations, accompanied by the consequent experience of loss of identity, has never been a pretty sight, not now nor at the time of the formation of that millenarian Jewish cult two thousand years ago, when what became Christianity was established as a compulsory state religion in the declining Roman Empire. Eternal life was offered to those who accepted Christianity, a novel and attractive prospect in a time of increasing uncertainty about the future. English historian Edward Gibbon in his *History of the Decline and Fall of the Roman Empire* attributed growing belief in Christianity as a factor in the profound changes that led to the end of the Western half of the empire, and the transformation of the Eastern half into a theocracy. A millennium after the fall of the Western Roman Empire and the triumph of the Christian world view, we again live in a time of impending social collapse, and it seems unlikely that Enlightenment values like reason will persist in the face of our human-caused extinction.

To be misanthropic may now seem inevitable. Every advance in science, apart from perhaps cosmology, has contributed to our human ability to destroy ourselves. But the issue is much more fundamental than that, for competition, promoting survival and reproduction, is manifested in all animal species. And this is not limited to animal or plant species. Nor does the process stop with even simpler quasi-living systems like viruses, which hijack the genetic machinery of more structured organisms with the sole aim of reproducing a genetic code to manufacture more virus. What we observe at all of these different levels of organization is clearly a general and universal concept of living systems, from the simplest to the most complex, all employing the same drives of survival and reproduction.

Arthur Schopenhauer's 1818 concept of *will*, never refuted, has instead been elaborated upon by Freud and others. Going well beyond simple misanthropy, or dislike of other people, it is a statement about what is contained in *all* living systems. This does not, however, preclude being kind to others, for we are all trapped in this same natural phenomenon called life.

August 2, 2021

120

Harbingers of Doom

Two articles appeared in summer 2020 foreshadowing the disheartening prospects for human civilization throughout the remaining eight decades of this century. In his essay "The Unraveling of America," published in the August 6, 2020, edition of *Rolling Stone*, anthropologist Wade Davis described the effect of the global COVID-19 pandemic on the fragile democracy of the United States, characterizing it as a "seminal event," a turning point in history that will cause mass economic uncertainty and collapse of "a failed state ruled by a dysfunctional and incompetent government."

Davis attributes this collapse to the hubris and greed associated with American exceptionalism, exemplified by their boasting of the president as the "leader of the free world." The explosion of urban violence, the opioid crisis, the brutal oppression of racial minorities, the lack of control of lethal weaponry and the celebration of the individual over the collective well-being together presage the end of the American experiment, a reminder that all kingdoms eventually collapse and empires wither away.

Polybius, a Greek historian of the Hellenistic period (around 200 BCE), wrote of the rotating cycle of society's political structures, from monarchy through ochlocracy (mob rule) and then back to monarchy. When societal unrest becomes intolerable, he observed, demands for a strong leader to restore order have always led to one arising, promising to set things straight. Thus Caesar, Bonaparte, Lenin, Mao, Hitler and assorted contemporary candidates like Trump or Putin surface from the ever-boiling pot of discontents.

But the cultural and political vicissitudes of one failing state fade into insignificance considering what "civilization" is doing to our planet. In the August 20, 2020, edition of the *New York Review of Books,* Bill McKibben reviewed Mark Lynas's *Our Final Warning: Six Degrees of Climate Emergency*, in which Lynas identifies the COVID-19 pandemic as a harbinger of an unfolding disastrous future in which a sequence of crises will inevitably overwhelm the coping abilities of our civilization.

Lynas succinctly outlines the consequences associated with each degree Celsius of global warming, including environmental damage, certain to increase exponentially to the point that life as we know it will no longer be possible and simple survival will eclipse all former concerns and amenities of living. Present-day political squabbles over "freedom" and "human rights" will become irrelevant when the primary concern becomes one of life or death. Lynas's careful stepwise delineation by degrees is not only a prognostication of our future. Each degree of increase brings new horrors. "The main question," he writes, "is whether we'll be able to hold the rise in temperature to a point where we can, at great expense and suffering, deal with those crises coherently, or whether they will overwhelm the coping abilities of our civilization." The latter is a distinct possibility, as Lynas makes painfully clear. Echoing this sentiment, McKibben writes of Lynas's work, "It's also a tour of hell."

We may howl with rage and gnash our teeth, trapped as we are in our self-made hell, and seek to assign blame to "science" or, inappropriately, to leaders considered to be personally responsible for our unhappy circumstances. With disorder continuing around us, individual discontent is understandable, and will doubtless become increasingly widespread as the pressures associated with climate change steadily and inevitably increase. Worldwide co-operation is a possible means of retarding, but not reversing, the effects of climate change. In other words, don't hold your breath.

Homo sapiens is ensuring its own destruction with the combined consequences of applied science and environmental destruction, arising from the Enlightenment, made possible by the industrial revolution and facilitated by the global capitalist economic systems promoting individual and corporate greed. The evolved development of consciousness in *Homo sapiens* has endowed our species with both the blessing and the curse of understanding our situation.

August 30, 2020; compiled with
"The Blessing and Curse of Reason," February 6, 2022

Since writing essay #120 exactly one year ago, nothing has happened, and so it goes, dire warning after dire warning, and driven by greed, the disaster continues to unfold. Humanity is doomed; self-destruction proceeds apace.

August 30, 2021

121

The Precipice

The Precipice: Existential Risk and the Future of Humanity by Oxford scholar and philosopher Toby Ord of the Future of Humanity Institute contains much to reflect on concerning realistic possible causes of future human extinction. Ord delineates two types of risks, natural and anthropogenic, or man-made. The former would be like the asteroid collision that extinguished the dinosaurs or the eruption of a supervolcano, casting a layer of soot in the atmosphere impenetrable to sunshine. While possible, these are not likely scenarios for human extinction, and Ord reckons that we should be good for another million years or so based on our geological history.

Anthropogenic causes are another matter. Ord considers nuclear war and its consequences, like fallout and "nuclear winter," as not necessarily entirely lethal to all life. Environmental degradation resulting from climate change, on the other hand, could conceivably lead to a runaway greenhouse effect leading to the boiling off of the oceans, making life impossible, as may have possibly have occurred on the planet Venus. While not completely negligible, Ord puts the chance of this occurring on our Earth at 0.1 percent.

For Ord, the greatest anthropogenic risks are those of "engineered pandemics" and artificial intelligence (AI). He estimates the former, resulting from biological error or terror, such as an accidental escape of a lethal organism or an intentional leak from a lab that synthesizes viral agents, has a 1 in 30 chance of ending human life on Earth. Above all, however, Ord feels the greatest risk to humans derives from AI, from rogue machines that can't be programmed to *only* serve our interests. Devising a machine that is always aligned with human values may not be possible, and Ord estimates that artificial intelligence has a 1 in 10 chance of ending human life on Earth, the highest of all knowns.

This is, of course, speculative, and there may be "unknown unknowns," such as alien invasions, high-energy physics experiments creating artificial black holes that can't be turned off, or other science-fiction doomsday scenarios. This speculation about possible ends of human existence raises philosophical and ethical issues: how much attention need we pay to mitigate existential risk by greater vigilance, safer technologies and international cooperation? For Ord, "relinquishing further technological progress is not a solution."

Not merely happiness but humanity's promise for achievement is what moves Ord, even though most of the time we don't consciously worry about whether humanity survives or not.

Still, the idea of a very distant extinction should not deter us from trying to prevent avoidable extinction in the nearer future. Our ability to experience worthwhile lives today is meaningful, and worthy of being pursued in the present and in the days that lie ahead.

March 11, 2021

122

AI: *Human Compatible* and Human Survival

Stuart Russell is a professor of computer science at the University of California, the coauthor of a textbook on artificial intelligence (AI), the winner of many academic awards, an advisor to governments and undeniably at the summit of his discipline. His acclaimed book *Human Compatible* is a lucid presentation of his views about intelligent machines and a breakdown of the avoidable risks they will pose.

In my opinion, Russell's book deserves to be read by that limited number of literate humans who express an interest in the future of our species on this ravaged planet, given the potential threats to our survival by application of known technological algorithms in diverse fields like extraction of non-renewable resources, population control, political advancement of the elite, warfare and the ultimate realization that success by superintelligent machines may not be compatible with the survival of the species. Alan Turing is quoted wondering in 1951, "If a machine can think, it might think more intelligently than we do, and then where should we be? ... This new danger ... is certainly something which can give us anxiety."

Russell's views of "huge potential benefits of AI, as well as the hazards and ethical challenges" have been described as reasons for hope by many eminent reviewers in the publisher's blurbs, but I believe that the prospect of self-directed weaponry in war remains the Achilles heel evident to anyone familiar with the history of military conflict. Every single invention of humanity, from catapults to dynamite to nuclear fission and possible biological weapons created by CRISPR gene editing of DNA in viruses, has been used, or has the potential of being used, to kill enemies in the service of success in military conflicts between opposing groups, and there is absolutely no reason to expect any different result in the future from employing AI in some form to ensure victory.

I am reminded of a cartoon in a *New Yorker* magazine back in 1954 depicting a small group of horrified observers at a nuclear test site, glaring accusingly at a trembling, white-coated participant replying to them, "Don't blame me, I'm only a scientist!" But it's not the scientist who deserves the blame, but rather what Kant called the "crooked timber of humanity."

Diplomacy and compromise are always preferable to warfare and must be encouraged whenever possible. Mutually assured destruction is and has been a powerful deterrent when employed by opposing powers, but inserting an AI-determined step to launch the missiles (or to initiate some other irreversible action) seems like a sinister prelude to a future dystopia.

March 26, 2021

123

Heat Death

Commonly used to represent the end point in a cosmological model based on the second law of thermodynamics, in which all available energy in the universe has been converted into heat and is therefore unavailable to do any work, the term *heat death* now resonates in the here and now of the twenty-first century as we face extended periods of uncomfortably elevated ambient temperatures around the world.

This is particularly noteworthy (at this time) in the northwestern portion of North America, where the population is unaccustomed to living in these extreme conditions. Those not able to artificially cool their surroundings by air conditioning are advised to visit "cooling centres" if needed, and if available in a nearby area, but this advice, while compassionate, is only a short-term solution, for it only adds to the artificial production of more heat by employing energy to run the machinery required to lower temperature. (Perhaps if the shareholders of the largest exploitative corporations didn't have air conditioning, we'd be in a different boat by now.)

The pursuit of the chimera of comfort by destruction of the environment is a good example of human niche construction as an evolutionary mechanism to enhance survival and reproduction. At the heart of such endeavours lies the prime mover: inborn greed, the love and competitive pursuit of money or other items representing value as a symbol of power and success among all other organisms. The manufacture, promotion and sale of machinery to change the local environment, as with heating and cooling systems, contributes to the phenomenon of global warming, a positive and now inescapable runaway feedback loop that will lead to the extinction of human "*sapiens.*"

Most of mankind lives only in the present, with individuals attempting to satisfy their own basic needs, while capitalists enrich the portfolios of those willing to satisfy these needs in exchange for cash. Human beings constantly employ entitlement as a reason to attain satisfaction, and the end point of this process will undeniably be the collapse of civilization, with governments unable to control armed mobs as they assert their "right" to control others as a way of securing possession of the means to acquire wealth.

A pervasive image is that of a horde of mindless rodents rushing towards their own self-destruction. Thermodynamics can wait for the end of the universe, but meanwhile we are creating our own little heat death. After we are gone, the mountains will remain, and over eons of time, another species may arise on this planet. Its success, however, like ours, will be dependent upon the same inborn biological drive towards survival and reproduction.

Like those of Schopenhauer, Freud and others, this belief is neither one of pessimism nor cynicism but simply realism, the understanding of which demands resilience in the mind of the observer. I concur with philosopher of science Herbert Feigl of the Vienna Circle, who avowed seeking not a dismissive "nothing but" or a metaphysical "something more," but only a descriptive "what is what" in thinking about nature and humanity.

June 28, 2021

124

If . . .

This short English word of but two letters may be used as a conjunction or as a noun. In the case of the former, it represents a conditional statement about the future and so is related to the dimension of time, a suggestion that "*if* (a), then (b)," as in "*if* you steal, then you may be charged with theft." As a noun, the word *if* is used to represent possible conditions of some future event. For example, one may assert "there are too many *ifs* associated with this condition to predict an outcome."

This little word has appeared often in accounts of the consequences of global warming, not only in popular media sources, such as the *Guardian Weekly,* but in sober assessments by scientists and other academics. According to the US's National Public Radio (NPR), one number was heard more than any other at the United Nations climate summit in Glasgow, Scotland: 1.5°C. While 1.5°C was the global climate change goal world leaders agreed to strive for by limiting carbon, these were merely "pledges," and pledges, of course, imply *ifs*. What is more, these recent pledges don't go far enough. The NPR segment noted, "Even with more ambitious emission cuts from some countries, warming is still on track for more than 2°C by the end of the century."

Environmental organizations lean heavily on hope when discussing or invoking possible means of minimizing the effects of global warming, such as through the replacement of fossil fuels with renewable resources like solar radiation and wind farms. The implication of these measures, however, have an attached *if*. Ignoring the inborn human drive to modify the biosphere by niche construction is probably an unattainable *if*. But the undeniable is rendered more palatable by the use of a conditional statement, sweetening a bitter truth by implying the possibility of a different outcome.

In any event, the damage has already been done and the expectation of catastrophic consequences to civilization, and the associated social instabilities, is unquestionable. Denial of this is simply whistling in the dark, and the gnashing of teeth and wringing of hands will no doubt be characteristic of the remaining years of the twenty-first century.

One of the few benefits of old age is that of not living long enough to be subjected to the anticipated consequences of human folly, but it is no consolation to imagine the level of suffering that will be experienced by others. There is no *if* associated with the coming collapse of civilization; it is only a matter of *when*.

November 6, 2021

125

Suicide, Metamorphosis and Global Warming

Committing violence against oneself has been seen by many world religions at different times as deserving of condemnation as a sin, an offence against God, the creator of life. Since it was seen as a destruction of life, itself a gift from God, those who committed suicide retained no body after death, letting the punishment fit the crime. For example, in *Inferno*, Book I of Dante's fourteenth-century epic poem *The Divine Comedy*, those who have committed the sin of suicide, thereby denying their bodily existence in life, are in death now only souls, appearing as gloomy wood and transformed into torn and broken plants and trees. This metamorphosis is consistent with the famous admonition displayed on the gated entrance to Dante's Hell: "Abandon hope all ye who enter."

Those damned were condemned to their existence in Hell for eternity, unlike those sinners in *Purgatorio*, Book II of the *Divine Comedy*, who were admitted to purgatory pending forgiveness, anticipating entrance to *Paradiso* in Book III.

Suicide as self-destruction was a recent topic of discussion by UK psychoanalyst and essayist Adam Phillips in the January 6, 2022, *London Review of Books*. His essay "On Giving Up" opens with a quote from Kafka: "From a certain point there is no more turning back." To me, this aphorism resonates with the year 2014, identified as the "point of no return" with respect to oceanic warming. According to the US Environmental Protection Agency, "Even if greenhouse gas emissions were stabilized tomorrow, it would take many more years — decades to centuries — for the oceans to adjust to changes in the atmosphere and the climate that have already occurred."

After another eight years of continued atmospheric heating, turning back now is no longer possible, and there is no alternative to giving up. The ignorance of those who deny global warming is self-evident. Appeals to limit carbon emissions are ignored, and while the promotion of recycling is commendable, it is ineffective. The most that can be expected now is to perhaps slow the rate of warming. There is no going back; the damage has already been done. We are not "passing through" a period of global warming, as recently characterized by a journalist, we are stuck in it. With no exit.

Homo "sapiens" have already passed through the gates of their own self-created Hell. Unlike in Dante's poem, there won't be any metamorphosis, and species suicide is unavoidable. Being dead is no problem, but the dying is bound to be hellish.

February 10, 2022

126

Of Hope, Despair and Detachment

Writing in *The Conversation* earlier this year, US essayist and academic Rachel Hadas cited classical authors in the context of maintaining a sense of hope that an end of the current viral pandemic was in sight. She believed that human beings are more enduring, more adaptable, than we give ourselves credit for, suggesting that in "Plato's allegory of the cave, Socrates suggests that any prisoner dragged forcibly out of the cave would feel pain and rage until he became acclimatized to the shadows, reflections, the stars and moon, and finally the light of the sun."

Perhaps so, but this pandemic is only one example in the never-ending struggle of living organisms, from the simple to the most complex, to achieve mastery over the external world through growth and reproduction. A Finnish proverb nicely illustrates this: "If you run away from a wolf, then a bear comes after you."

Viruses and bacteria replicate, or reproduce, as do all other living organisms, including mammals like *Homo sapiens*. Competition is a universal characteristic of all living beings, giving rise to the idea that life itself could be thought of as a kind of "disease" that affects that part of nature devoid of living matter, places that may have the chemical ingredients but not living organisms that metabolize and replicate.

After the respiratory viral pandemic of COVID-19 winds down, there will be no future status quo ante, or return to normal, unless by *normal* is meant war or anarchic lawlessness. Other pandemics will arise. There never was any peaceful Eden, though for a few lucky enough, their childhood may have seemed like something similar in retrospect.

With increasing planetary desertification and the contraction of sustainable living spaces due to global warming, conflict is certain, and the inevitability of future wars among and between humans is beyond question. The resulting physical destruction, economic failures, starvation, enraged passions, cruelties and blame will no doubt provoke the collapse of what we deem "civilization."

To maintain a hopeful attitude now about the future suggests ignorance of the bellicose history of our species and a denial of what lies ahead. Marx knew this when he wrote in the mid-nineteenth century, "The past lies like a nightmare upon the present." Our present will become tomorrow's past, and our current temporary period of political quasi-stability will be thought enviable in the coming years of social turmoil by comparison.

The environmental crisis caused by human exploitation of the natural world is the leading current issue, but it is only a side effect of underlying competitiveness, a fundamental characteristic of all living matter. In this sense we can think of life in general as being a condition of the physical universe, whose evolution has led to our consciousness and awareness of who and what we are, of what we are doing to the world around us, and of what will be the likely result of our existence on the planet — extinction.

But the absence of hope does not necessarily imply the presence of despair. A stoic resignation, more characteristic of Eastern than Christian thought, suggests the existence of a neutral state without either hope or hopelessness. Withdrawal or detachment evades the dichotomy of hope and despair, but it remains an individual, not a social, goal and does nothing to ward off the multiple horrors awaiting our unfortunate descendants as our inborn drives assert their nature.

October 17, 2021

127

Facing the Future

There is no conceivable possibility of now reversing the environmental changes caused by human activity in the past few hundred years, which will lead to the sixth extinction of life on Earth. Some call out in despair for "ecological Leninism," the physical destruction of pipelines and other fossil fuel extractive industries, mobilizing their rage against capitalism into direct action. Others may turn to the distraction of entertainment, the false promises of religious cults, or the individual solace of psychoactive chemicals like opioids and psychedelics. Some no doubt will choose suicide, the deliberate destruction of their own consciousness.

Though not considered a Stoic, the Greek philosopher Epicurus recommended diversion from morbid thinking, focusing on moments in the past when one was most happy. Viktor Frankl, an Austrian psychiatrist and philosopher, and survivor of the Holocaust, wrote about employing this technique during his experiences in the Theresienstadt concentration camp. Ataraxia, or equanimity, a state of not being troubled by adversity, a state somewhat uncommon among mortal men and women, was an ideal of ancient Stoic philosophers. Its opposite, in comparison, manifested by wrath or rage, is incessantly displayed in today's media, both printed and online.

To be a good Stoic and to have ataraxia as a worthy goal may be desirable, but to achieve it in practice is often difficult. To perceive and admit one's own failings is uncomfortable, and to admonish others displaying wrath by advising them to be resilient, or to "lighten up," is generally resented as unwanted advice.

The eloquent and respected Canadian physician Sir William Osler (1849–1919) perspicaciously wrote, "The best way to develop a good sense of equanimity is not to expect too much from the people among whom you dwell." Fair enough. Just be kind if you can, and don't fret if you're not appreciated.

In the December 17, 2018, edition of the e-zine *Aeon,* scholar Alexander Wynne suggested Buddhist teachings as a way of achieving equanimity. Wynne began by summarizing what is known about the sage known as the Buddha ("the Awakened"), who emerged from a small town on the border between India and Nepal in the fifth century BCE. His early years are obscured by myth, but historical sources suggest he founded an austere cult based on meditation and the withdrawal from the vicissitudes of ordinary life. He taught a "dialectic of silence" and avoided engaging in speculation about issues such as the meaning of life, the relationship of man to nature, or issues of morality and instead cherished the virtues of a state of equanimity — mental or emotional stability or composure, calmness, equilibrium.

Buddhism has influenced Western culture since at least the nineteenth century, not only in fiction, like the novels of Herman Hesse, but more recently in the 1979 opera *Satyagraha* by Philip Glass, which references non-violence as a mode of confronting external threats. Wynne suggests the Buddhist approach of regarding the world as dependent on the activity of our minds and sense facilities could be considered "a useful aid to modern cognitive science." One wonders how so, this type of research becoming increasingly irrelevant to concerns of individual survival.

In psychology, mindfulness meditation, a mental training technique claiming to slow down racing thoughts, assist one in letting go of negativity and calm both the mind and body, is a form of psychological escapism akin to suicide, though non-lethal. The technique, derived from fairly recent Burmese innovations, is a therapeutic approach to subjective distress caused by life's problems. Although meditation was initially presented as an alternative to psychotropic medication, recent work in psychedelic facilitation of equanimity has led to the increased use of agents like psilocybin and lysergic acid.

Compiled from the essays "Ataraxia," February 4, 2021, and "Buddhism and Mindfulness," December 30, 2020; revised August 29, 2021

128

Feline Philosophy

An impressive amount of understanding about the observed behaviour of pussycats can be freely gathered from available resources on the internet, especially in revealing the ways they communicate, without language, in a variety of modalities, such as posture, tactile movements, vocalization and appearance.

English philosopher John Gray asks a question directed at humans: what can we learn about *ourselves* from our feline companions? In his short book *Feline Philosophy: Cats and the Meaning of Life,* Gray explores this idea, reviewing what earlier thinkers like Montaigne and Schopenhauer had to say on the matter. Gray writes, "When turned on itself, consciousness stands in the way of a good life .... Cats do not doubt that life is worth living. Human self-consciousness has produced the perpetual unrest that philosophy has vainly tried to cure." Cats, on the other hand, do not struggle to be happy; they just take life as it comes. Ethics does not trouble them; they are not empathic by nature and selfless egoism seems to suit them.

Feline selflessness has something in common with Zen Buddhism, in that a cat is fully absorbed in what it is doing at any one time, a state that is only intermittent in humans, as perhaps when playing a musical instrument, rock climbing or composing essays. Cats may take pleasure in our company and in playing with us, but they do not need us for amusement and are indifferent when we go away. They are not necessarily unresponsive, but rather express their emotions through their ears and tails, sometimes even by purring.

Unlike humans, cats do not kill for ideology. And as predators, they kill prey to eat (though they may appear to play with their food), not because they seek status, power or some kind of immortality. Gray writes, "There are no feline suicide warriors. When cats want to die it is because they no longer want to live." He also quotes philosopher Wittgenstein, who wrote, "If by eternity is understood not endless temporal duration but timelessness, then he lives eternally who lives in the present."

Gray suggests that to live like a cat means not taking into account anything beyond the life you lead. Forget about seeking the chimera of wisdom; it's a distraction from living, like the pursuit of happiness.

Cogito ergo sum, sed patior quod cogito.

That's all, folks. *La commedia è finita.*

December 24, 2020; revised November 18, 2021

129

The Conundrum of Literary Depressogenesis

As I edit this final section of essays, its grim contents about the futures of mankind and the planet are assaulting my normal sense of equanimity, inducing a state of depressed mood, clearly reactive and not endogenous. Perhaps I should see a psychiatrist.

But I am a psychiatrist. So then, should I look in a mirror? Aye, that's the conundrum.

An apocalyptic end to civilization is foreseen by pundits around the world. Not only has the popular press, like the BBC and the *Guardian,* sounded alarms, but academic essays and reports from international conferences of learned scientists concur that we are indeed living in the "end times." We can rage, rage, against the dying of the Enlightenment, but Auden quietly hushes Dylan, counselling us to "leave all love and hopes behind; out of sight is out of mind."

The madhouses and asylums are gone now, and while the halfway house where I lurk may be a refuge of sorts, it is no consolation. Writing, however, can be a form of therapy, externalizing one's fears by means of pen and paper (or keyboard and printer). The following therapeutic step would be to burn the inked laments, scatter the ashes and have another beer.

But first I'll read a few more chapters in Ezekiel to cheer myself up while sweating on my stationary bike to get the blood moving, before returning to complete the onerous task of editing my pandemic prose.

For it is also written in scripture that all is vanity and there is nothing new under the sun. Or in the contemporary immortal words of Alfred E. Neuman, "What, me worry?"

December 5, 2022

130

Snowdrops

In characterizing moods associated with flowers, snowdrops traditionally have suggested hope. They appear at the end of winter, before the vernal equinox, and so are seen as harbingers announcing the approach of springtime. This seems like an appropriate sentiment for the winter season, as hours of daylight noticeably increase forty-five days after the winter solstice. December's darkest days come before the holidays and the calendar year's end in the northern hemisphere. (Astronomically speaking, the more secular Chinese New Year, followed by the Spring Festival, seems like a more relevant annual event.)

Each year I watched the birch tree outside my former office window begin to bud and leaf out in March, and the earlier reminder of snowdrops was always a welcome sign of anticipation. While I know, approaching my tenth decade, that I could drop dead at any time and have accordingly gotten my "affairs in order," anticipating the return of each spring is still an annual pleasure, even though it is now accompanied by the poignant recognition of it perhaps being my last. But then that is true for all seasonal events that draw one's attention to intervals of time as duration, illuminating the contrast between subjective and standard times, the former with awareness of rapidly unfolding days and the latter with annually recurrent events like civic and religious holidays.

Many animals, like cats, continually live in the present, unaware of our arbitrary seasonal divisions. Our human awareness is the price we pay for having tasted of the apple of reason. Without this curse of looking for reasons to explain how things work, other animals just exist, living their lives in the present, perhaps culminating in reproduction, after which the remainder of their lives is essentially spent coasting, surviving, or maybe even behaving in ways to enhance the survival of other members of their species.

In thanks for a small donation last year, I was sent a little packet of wildflower seeds by the palliative care unit at a local hospital and seeded them in a small container on the sunny balcony of my flat. All summer long I enjoyed their silent but cheerful daily greetings until, overpowered by relentless cold and darkness in December, they slept their apparent lifeless slumber. But lo, the snowdrops today remind us they are awakening again, their pairs of white petals like two hands offering a silent prayer of thanks to sunshine and warmth, proclaiming the approach of yet another springtime.

Life goes on.

February 5, 2021

EPILOGUE

Consolation

These brief essays represent scattered thoughts about issues and ideas that have seemed interesting to me throughout a long life filled with many detours of attention. They are not intended to assert any universal truth or significance. Although these are only personal reflections, they may be of interest to others who are curious about one person's understanding of the ultimate issues of these twilight years of a civilization rapidly approaching its end.

As a final statement, while I believe that the future of humanity is certain extinction, and that there is no intrinsic "meaning" associated with the existence of any one human being, it has nevertheless been my good fortune to have had the opportunity of attempting to understand how we have come to be who and what we are, our origin and existence as conscious entities with individual, brief flashes of light — bright meteors in an otherwise dark cosmos.

This is my consolation.

ACKNOWLEDGEMENTS

In addition to the usual suspects of my few remaining supportive friends and many family members, wise editor Jessica Kaplan, and the diligent team at Granville Island Publishing, I will name only three writers among the legions in the past who have inspired me to continue sharing my thoughts in these short essays: Roman poet Lucretius (99–55 BCE) whose long poem *On the Nature of Things* led me as a teenager seventy years ago to love natural science and reason; Arthur Schopenhauer, the German philosopher and author of *The World as Will and Representation* (1818) that endowed me with a framework of understanding; and the twentieth-century Welsh author Jan Morris, who seasoned my sometimes grim thoughts with her salt of kindliness.

INDEX

Insatiability (Witkiewicz), 108
insults, 98
intelligence quotient (IQ) tests, 45–46
Intergovernmental Panel on Climate
    Change (IPCC), 191, 200
internet, 24
intuitionist mathematics, 156
Islam, 66
isms, 107
isolation, 102–103

J

Jack Reacher (character), 139
Jana, Smarajit, 41–42
Janus Point, The (Barbour), 19, 196
Jefferson, Thomas, 117
Jennens, Charles, 70
Jenner, Edward, 40
John the Baptist, 74
Johnson, Samuel, 116
Joule, James Prescott, 18–19
Joyce, James, 153
Judaism, 66, 68–69
Judt, Tony, 108–109
    Ill Fares the Land, 169
    Postwar, 178
Jupiter, 5
justice, 110–113
justice system (Canada), 95–96

K

K——, 94–95
Kalevala (Lönnrot), 141
Kallman, Chester, 99
Kant, Immanuel, 78, 96, 113, 115, 132,
    168–169, 187, 207
    Critique of Practical Reason, 132
Kepler, Johannes, 14
Kesey, Ken, *One Flew Over the Cuckoo's
    Nest,* 100–101
ketman, 108
Kingsnorth, Paul
    Alexandria, 173, 197–199
    Beast, 174–176, 198–199
    The Wake, 165–166, 175, 198–199
Kivi, Aleksis, 141
Knausgård, Karl Ove, 187
knights errant, 139–140
Kochenov, Dimitry, *Citizenship,* 124–125
Kullervo, 140–142

L

Laland, Kevin, 32–33
language learning, 1–2, 150

languages, 103, 149–150, 165–166
Last Letters from Hav (Morris), 159–160
last words, 187–188
Latin America, 126
laws of thermodynamics, 18–19
Le Guin, Ursula, 160
Lehrer, Tom, 198–199
Leibniz, Gottfried Wilhelm, 30
Lem, Stanislav, 34
Leskanich, Alexandre, 164
"Lessons of History, The" (Berlin), 107
Lewis Carroll, 150
LGBTQ community, and the HIV
    epidemic, 39
life, 196, 199, 202
life expectancy, 193
Life of Reason (Santayana), 112, 164
Liu, Cixin, *Alien Listening,* 15–16
Locke, John, 168–169
Lönnrot, Elias, *Kalevala,* 141
Lovelace, Richard, 182
Lovelock, James, 16, 200
LSD, 83–85
Luther, Martin, 74
Luyten, Willem, 12
Lynas, Mark, *Our Final Warning,*
    203–204

M

"Machine Stops, The" (Forster), 86
Mack, Katie, *The End of Everything,*
    21–22, 31, 157
McKibben, Bill, 203–204
Mad, Sad or Bad, 99–101
Mahler, Gustav, 102
Maier, Jessica, *The Eternal City,* 162–163
Malleus Maleficarum, 63–64
Malm, Andreas
    How to Blow Up a Pipeline, 190
    White Skin, Black Fuel, 190
Mandarin Chinese, 1–2
Manguel, Alberto, 30
manifest destiny, 125–127
Mann, Thomas, 135
Marani, Diego, *God's Dog,* 71–72
Marcus Tullius Cicero, 114–115
Margulis, Lynn, 16, 200
Mars, 5
Marvel, Kate, 192
Marx, Karl, 213
    *The Eighteenth Brumaire of Louis
        Napoleon,* 170
mathematical discoveries, 55–56
mathematical languages, 156

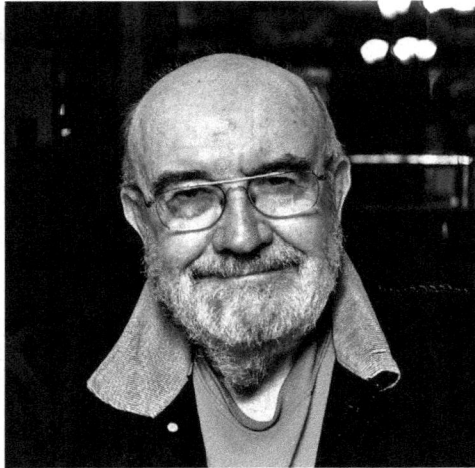

Jaime Smith, MD, FRCPC, was born in Appleton, Wisconsin. Upon completing his undergraduate studies in humanities at the University of Minnesota, Smith moved to Argentina to work as an astronomer at the national observatory, leaving behind the political framework of a country that he no longer supported.

Smith's path would ultimately lead him to British Columbia, where he was a university teacher in physics, mathematics and astronomy before changing careers and receiving his MD, followed by four years of training in psychiatry at the University of British Columbia. He has published two previous books, *Foxtrot* (2020) and *Stardust* (2021).

Smith was a participant in the fight to destigmatize homosexuality within the medical community and served on the front line of the AIDS epidemic in Vancouver, BC. A widower since 2011, he has three daughters, seven grandsons and four great-grandchildren.

To read more of Jaime's writing, visit his website: www.karhunluola.wordpress.com

www.ingramcontent.com/pod-product-compliance
Lightning Source LLC
Chambersburg PA
CBHW072123270326
41931CB00010B/1648